THE
JEWELRY MAKER'S
FIELD GUIDE
• Tools and Essential Techniques •

HELEN I. DRIGGS

INTERWEAVE
interweave.com

EDITOR
Marlene Blessing

TECHNICAL EDITOR
Jane Dickerson

TECHNICAL REVIEWER
Mark Nelson

ASSOCIATE ART DIRECTOR
Julia Boyles

COVER & INTERIOR DESIGN
Adrian Newman

PHOTOGRAPHER
Jim Lawson

PRODUCTION DESIGNER
Katherine Jackson

© 2013 Helen Driggs

Photography & Illustrations
© 2013 Interweave

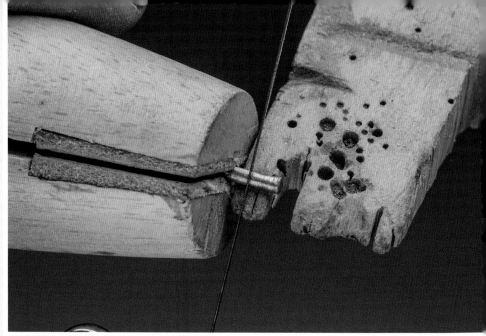

Interweave
A division of F+W Media, Inc.
201 East Fourth Street
Loveland, CO 80537
interweave.com

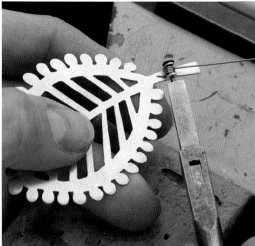

Manufactured in China by
RR Donnelley Shenzhen

Library of Congress Cataloging-
in-Publication Data

Driggs, Helen I.

The jewelry maker's field guide :
tools and essential techniques /

Helen I. Driggs.

   pages cm

Includes bibliographical references
and index.

ISBN 978-1-59668-976-3 (pbk)
ISBN 978-1-59668-908-4 (PDF)

1. Jewelry making--Handbooks,
manuals, etc. 2. Jewelry
making--Equipment and supplies.
I. Title.

TT212.D75 2013

745.594'2--dc23

2013009032

10 9 8 7 6 5 4 3 2 1

ACKNOWLEDGMENTS

Every life that touches yours will form your way of being; the person you are at any moment in time exists because of a web of connections with others. I am grateful for my rich, full and rewarding life of connections. True happiness is found on an individual path and in finding a purpose. I am lucky to be in that place at this time.

Many of my colleagues worked with me on this book, and many thanks to all of them. It is impossible here for me to express my gratitude to every person I would like to: however, some deserve special recognition:

To my teachers: thank you for sharing your knowledge with me;

To my family, here and not: thank you for supporting my dreams;

To my son: thank you for making me feel unbearably proud;

To Michael Boyd: thank you for an undemanding friendship without a hidden agenda;

To Merle White: thank you for trusting me;

To Jaime Carvajal Farfan: thank you for loving me.

Helen I. Driggs

January 2013

CONTENTS

INTRODUCTION:
How to Use This Book

This is a book about jeweler's tools and the many and varied techniques connected with each. All artists have their own preferences. Some tools are general and universal: typically, every jeweler owns a saw, files, torch, flex shaft, and a few basic hammers. After that, each individual artist's tool choices relate to the work he or she prefers to create.

ADD ONE TOOL AT A TIME

It can be quite expensive to outfit a workshop fully. Most often, tools are added to an artist's shop on an as-needed basis. My own workshop has taken nearly a decade to equip, and there are still several pieces of equipment I do not yet own. The best advice I can offer about tools is to purchase only what you need as you need it. Spend wisely on your tools, use them for some time to become familiar with them before you buy more tools, and save money for metal—otherwise, you will have nothing on which to use those tools.

LEARN IN STAGES

I have organized this book in the sequence a first-year metals student would learn the craft. It is ordered by tool and material categories, which are illustrated and for which I describe their various uses. Cross-references throughout the text will guide you to related information. It is important for you to understand what a tool is used for, as well as how to use it correctly to protect both yourself and the tool.

Patience and willingness to practice are perhaps the two most important skills for an aspiring jeweler to learn. Take time to read each section and work slowly, patiently, and carefully. Following the applied techniques will familiarize you with a particular tool group. Then you will practice using the tool in a guided lesson. Both your hands and your eyes will become educated and more precise as you work through the lessons. If you don't get something the first time around, try again.

Making jewelry is fun: it is easy to be swept away by your enthusiasm. The tendency to rush work to completion is difficult to control; but well-made, beautifully finished, and aesthetically pleasing jewelry takes time to create. There are no shortcuts. Put the thought of jewelry to wear out of your head and focus instead on each task in its turn. Such discipline will help you control the desire to rush before you should. The reward for your patience will be an enduring object of beauty and, ultimately, mastery of the skills you need to create many more.

Learn from Front to Back

Follow the first eight building blocks in this book and you will develop the foundation skills you need for a long and fascinating trip through the process of jewelry making. I recommend that you try every set of applied techniques in the order they are presented, as each builds important skills for you that are interconnected.

BUILD A FOUNDATION

Some areas of technique will appeal to you more than others: this is natural. But it is important to develop the skill sets presented in each of the first eight building blocks before you mix them up into functional forms of your own design. As you practice, you will see improvements in your skills. So save your early attempts—nothing is more satisfying than witnessing your own evolution.

Work hard, work safe, and may the gods of metal smile upon you!

PART ONE:
Raw Materials

Cross-reference: *Universal Gauge Chart, page 34*

When it comes to which metal you choose for making jewelry, there are so many options. You can construct wearable art from **precious** and **base metals** and their **alloys**, **ferrous** or **nonferrous metals**, and recycled or reclaimed metals.

JEWELRY METALS AND ALLOYS

Each type of metal has its own advantages and limitations: a property that presents an insurmountable problem for one artist may be chosen by another for this very property. Do not let the potential difficulty of using a particular metal dissuade you from using it, because creative or innovative design solutions typically emerge from working around a problem. Every material has the potential to become an interesting ingredient in studio jewelry.

Proper studio material management in the beginning will pay off in the long run. So take the time to document and label everything as you acquire it to avoid costly errors once you get caught up in the work. It is important to store and label all metal by recording the material, price paid, and source, especially for alloys. Many metals look similar and are easy to confuse when they are placed side by side. However, each supplier or mill has a proprietary "recipe" for each metal alloy it produces, which may or may not be evident until the metals are worked.

When you purchase metal from the mill or supply house, you will need to decide on three things:

- type of metal
- form of the metal: **gauge** or shape
- dimensions or weight of the metal

Depending on the supplier and the metal, the costs are tied to fluctuations of the daily metals market prices. Once you have chosen your metal type and decided how much of it you want, you'll multiply its weight by the **spot price** for that day.

When purchasing metal, it is important to ask what the daily price is. A supplier will either add in or subtract out of the advertised base price relative to the actual daily price—or, spot price—at that moment or on that day.

Most suppliers offer a cutting service for stock or sheet and will charge a nominal per-cut fee to subdivide the purchased metal into smaller dimensions once you have purchased the minimum size. It is often well worth paying a cutting fee for small or oddly shaped subdivisions of sheet because you will save time in doing so.

Types of metals

NOBLE or **PRECIOUS METALS** are lustrous and very resistant to corrosion and oxidation. In the jewelry industry, they are typically referred to as precious metals and include gold, platinum, and silver. Other precious metals include members of the platinum group: ruthenium, rhodium, palladium, osmium, and iridium, some of which are used in precious-metal alloys and for plating sterling silver to reduce tarnishing.

FERROUS METALS contain iron or steel. Historically, they were not often used for making jewelry up until the industrial revolution, when they were introduced in the mass manufacture of costume jewelry components and as completed jewelry pieces. Since the 1970s, both iron and steel have become more commonly used in studio jewelry, particularly iron and stainless steel. Hot-forged iron or steel is worked using blacksmithing techniques, while stainless steel is machined or milled because it is extremely hard to fabricate using only hand tools. Both iron and steel are difficult to join by **soldering** and are typically welded together instead, which creates a visible seam where the parts coalesce. An easy way to identify most iron or steel is to use a magnet; plus, with the exception of stainless steel, these metals will rust when wet—typically they must be sealed with lacquer, polymer, or wax when used for jewelry.

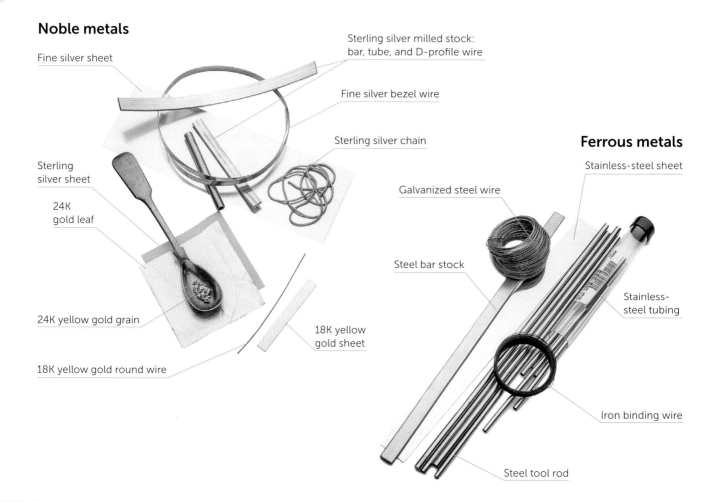

Noble metals

Fine silver sheet

Sterling silver milled stock: bar, tube, and D-profile wire

Fine silver bezel wire

Sterling silver chain

Sterling silver sheet

24K gold leaf

24K yellow gold grain

18K yellow gold sheet

18K yellow gold round wire

Ferrous metals

Stainless-steel sheet

Galvanized steel wire

Steel bar stock

Stainless-steel tubing

Iron binding wire

Steel tool rod

NONFERROUS METALS include aluminum, titanium, and niobium—the **reactive** and **transitional metals** commonly used in jewelry. Nonferrous metals do not contain iron or steel and do not rust. Sometimes called **"space-age"** or, in the case of titanium and niobium, **refractory metals**, they are light and strong and their surfaces can be oxidized to take on a rainbow of vibrant colors when **anodized**. Aluminum is very soft and therefore melts at low temperatures. It forms surface **oxides** very rapidly, making it difficult to solder well; low-temperature solder must be used.

Titanium is very hard and difficult to fabricate, but is typically hypoallergenic: historically it has been used in dentistry and medicine for implants and surgical devices. It is often machined but can be commercially cast. Niobium is used in many steel alloys, but has become popular on its own in jewelry since the 1970s because it is strong, light, forms rich and beautiful colors when anodized, and is rarely allergenic. All three of these metals are widely used for assembled jewelry such as chain or **maille**, and as manufactured links, units, and components.

BASE METAL is an old and common industrial term used for abundant and inexpensive metals, as opposed to the noble—or precious—metals, which were mainly gold and silver. Typically these metals oxidize when exposed to air or moisture. Examples of base metals for jewelry include nickel, nickel alloys, tin, and zinc. Copper is also considered a base metal because it oxidizes rapidly. Copper base-metal alloys include **monel metal**, brass, and bronze. Modern pewter is a tin alloy (unlike traditional, lead-based pewter) that is also used for jewelry: it is very soft and melts at low temperatures.

Reactive metals

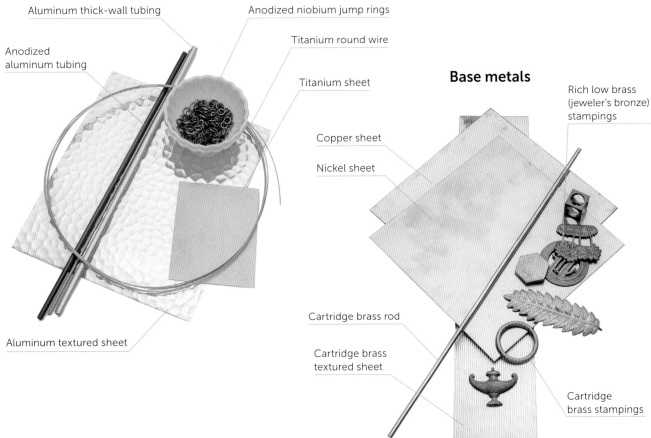

Aluminum thick-wall tubing

Anodized aluminum tubing

Anodized niobium jump rings

Titanium round wire

Titanium sheet

Aluminum textured sheet

Base metals

Rich low brass (jeweler's bronze) stampings

Copper sheet

Nickel sheet

Cartridge brass rod

Cartridge brass textured sheet

Cartridge brass stampings

Because of its low-melt characteristics, casting, **repoussé**, and forming are typical fabrication methods for pewter.

Many artists work with or create their own custom alloys and **SPECIALTY METALS**, such as **reticulation silver** (80 percent silver and 20 percent copper), which forms interesting textures after repeated heatings. Bonded or laminated metal sheets called **bi-metals** allow an artist to feature two colors of metal on one surface. A Korean metals technique called **keum-boo** features 24K gold leaf bonded to silver and is quite beautiful. Copper bonded to silver creates exciting patterns and design potential when used in tandem with a patina. Japanese metalworkers first developed several unique alloys and processes that are very popular in modern studio jewelry. **Mokumé-gane** is a process by which layers of various metals and alloys are laminated and then manipulated with tools to produce a wide variety of patterns that resemble wood grain. **Shakudo** is a well-known Japanese alloy of gold and copper and is popular and noteworthy because of the beautiful purple patina it can produce. **Shibuichi** is another alloy from Japan: it is produced by alloying three-fourths copper to one-fourth silver. **Filled metals** contain a core of brass, **jeweler's bronze**, or other metal. A thick overlay of the designated metal covers the core. For example, 14K yellow gold–filled metal is a core of brass coated with 14K gold. Usually, a notation reveals the ratio of the precious metal as a part of the total weight: for example, 1/20 14K means 5 percent of the total weight is gold.

Measuring metal

In the United States, nonferrous metals are measured using the Brown and Sharpe (B & S) system, also known as the American Standard and American Wire Gauge (AWG). This tool may also be purchased in Europe as the Standard Wire Gauge (SWG), which is sanctioned by the British Board of Trade. One of the first tools I recommend purchasing is the **B & S GAUGE** for sheet and wire.

Specialty metals

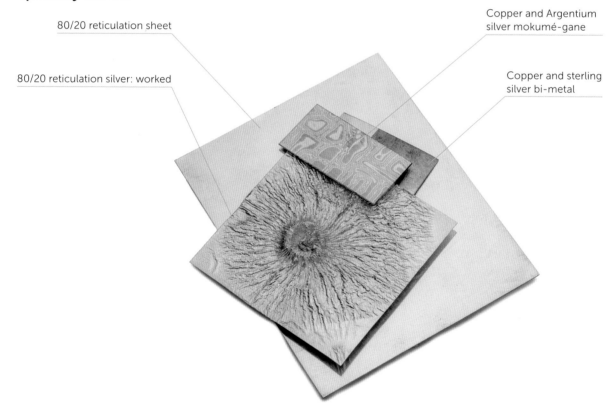

80/20 reticulation sheet

80/20 reticulation silver: worked

Copper and Argentium silver mokumé-gane

Copper and sterling silver bi-metal

This gauge shows wire gauge on one side and decimal or millimeter equivalents on the reverse side. The larger the number, the thinner the metal.

Another important measuring tool is a **spring divider**, used for dividing and transferring measurements to metal in combination with rulers, templates, and squares.

The last essential measuring tool is a high-quality **tempered steel ruler** that is delineated with inches down to $\frac{1}{32}$ on one side and with decimal amounts down to millimeters on the other. Often, these rulers will display a table of fractions with their decimal equivalents on the reverse side.

Weighing metal

Depending on the type and form of metal you select, you will need to be aware of weight in addition to dimensions. Three different measurement systems come into play when working with metal and it is important to be able to make conversions within each measurement system as well as between them.

TROY WEIGHT is used to measure precious metals:

- 24 grains = 1 pennyweight (dwt.)
- 20 dwt. = 1 troy ounce
- 12 troy ounces = 1 troy pound (5,760 grains)

AVOIRDUPOIS WEIGHT is used to measure base metals:

- 16 drams = 1 ounce avoirdupois
- 16 ounces = 1 pound avoirdupois (256 drams)
- To convert ounces troy to ounces avoirdupois, multiply by 1.09714.
- To convert ounces avoirdupois to ounces troy, multiply by 0.91146.

GRAM WEIGHTS are used in the metric system.
- 1 gram = 15.43 grains troy
- 3.888 grams = 1 dram
- 1.555 grams = 1 pennyweight (dwt.)
- 31.104 grams = 1 troy ounce
- 28.35 grams = 1 ounce avoir

Measuring tools

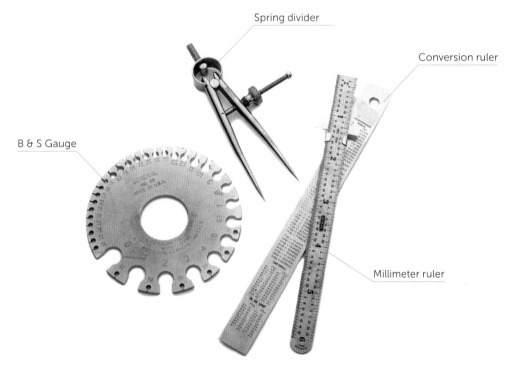

Spring divider

Conversion ruler

B & S Gauge

Millimeter ruler

Metal forms

Every supplier has a wide selection of different metal and metal forms from which to choose. Some specialize in a certain type of metal; others deal in a wide variety of shapes, metals, and forms. Weighing and measuring metal is done using a standardized system and is mandated by law in whatever country you purchase it. Once you have determined the type of metal you want to use, the next step is to decide how much you need, what form would be the best one to start with—based on the design of the intended jewelry object, and what technique you will use to fabricate it. Most suppliers have a minimum size requirement for every form of metal they sell, so it is important to keep those sizes in mind when purchasing to avoid additional fees.

SHEET is the most common starting point for many fabricated objects and is thus the most widely purchased form of metal. Because sheet metal is malleable, it is very versatile and can be pieced, pierced, formed, folded, and joined by soldering. Sheet can be patterned or plain. It is measured by gauge and dimensions, then weighed and priced according to the daily metal market or spot price.

INGOTS are dense, unformed blocks of a particular metal or metal alloy that can be transformed into sheet by rolling and compressing in a mill. Ingots can also be forged or formed directly with hammers and stakes; carved or engraved; or cut into small sections, melted, and cast. Ingots are purchased by weight.

Sheet metal

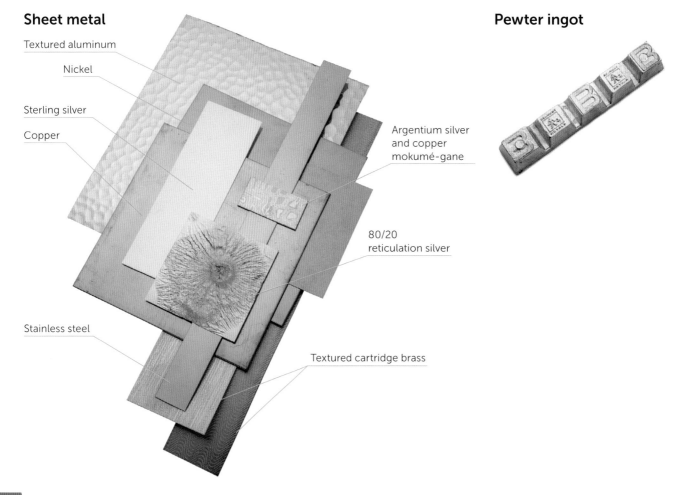

Textured aluminum

Nickel

Sterling silver

Copper

Argentium silver and copper mokumé-gane

80/20 reticulation silver

Stainless steel

Textured cartridge brass

Pewter ingot

MILLED STOCK includes specialty metal forms such as rod, bar, strip, tubing, discs, rings or loops, patterned or gallery wire or stock, and other common components. Milled stock is a tremendous time-saver because it is available in forms that would otherwise take considerable time to fabricate from scratch. It is measured by gauge and/or dimensions in inches or millimeters, plus length in inches or feet, and is then weighed and priced according to the daily metal market or spot price.

GRAIN and **PELLETS** are used for casting. Most grain has been measured and alloyed, mixed, and then melted into very small pellets or freeform pieces, such as chunks. Often, additives and antioxidation chemicals are added to the alloy to reduce oxidation, give uniform color, and cause the molten metal to flow into the mold efficiently. Grain and pellets are purchased by weight.

WIRE is widely available and comes in several shapes, including round, half-round, square, rectangle, triangle, and patterned. Like sheet, wire is very versatile and can be pieced, formed, woven, and joined by soldering. It is measured by gauge and length in inches or feet, then weighed and priced according to the daily metal market or spot price. Base metal wire is typically purchased by the coil or spool and is most commonly priced per pound.

Milled stock

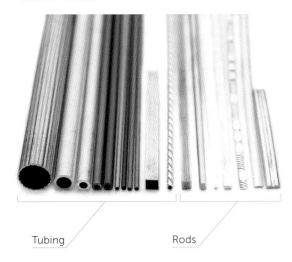

Tubing   Rods

Wire

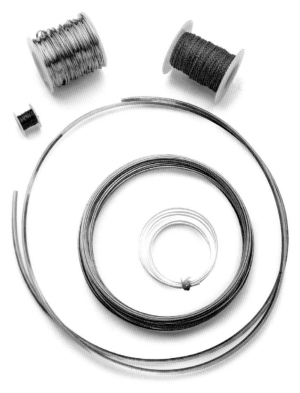

Bronze casting grain

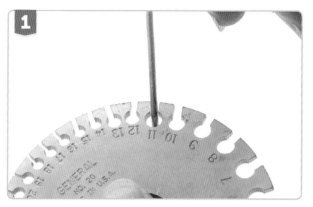

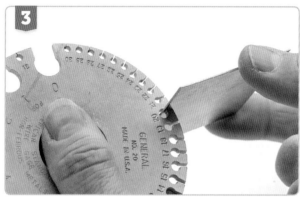

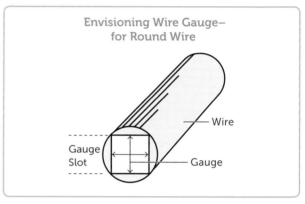

Envisioning Wire Gauge— for Round Wire

Wire

Gauge Slot

Gauge

How to use the B & S gauge

You will notice this gauge has slots that end in circular openings: but don't make the mistake of thinking the circles have anything to do with measuring, because they don't. They are there to allow a metal sheet edge or a wire to be inserted past the entire slot for measuring accuracy. The slots are what determine the true gauge. For all metals and wire, do not attempt to gauge them close to an edge that may have been compressed by a shear or cutter. The truest gauge measurement will be taken near an edge that has been sawn.

FOR WIRE. Insert the wire into the slot you estimate is nearest its diameter. It should slide in and out easily without catching. Move to the next smallest slot. If the wire

inserts partially, but not fully, that is the gauge to choose, because the mass of the round wire is greater in the center, and you are sliding into an opening with straight sides.

To envision the wire gauge, imagine a thin, circular slice of the wire. The actual gauge of the round wire would be the diameter of a true square placed within the circle as shown (above).

1. Measure round wire accurately by comparing it in two adjacent slots on the wire gauge. If the wire slides freely in and out of the slot, the actual gauge wire is smaller. *(Fig 1)*

2. Test the wire in the next smallest gauge. If the wire does not slide into the slot fully, choose that gauge as the true diameter of the wire. *(Fig. 2)*

FOR SHEET. Insert the cut edge into the slot you estimate is nearest its diameter. Again, it should slide easily in and out without catching. Move to the next smallest slot. If the sheet inserts partially, but not fully, go back to the next largest slot of the gauge. It is important to slide the sheet all the way through the slot into the circular opening of the gauge. If it is difficult to decide the true gauge of the sheet, I recommend that you err on the side of the thinner gauge: it is easier to remove metal than to add it. A too-thick gauge sheet can be made thinner in the rolling mill, but not the opposite.

3. Insert metal sheet fully into the tool slot for the most accurate assessment of the gauge. *(Fig. 3)*

Quick Notation System for Metals

I use the periodic table of the elements as my guide to mark my metal, no matter what form it is. I always record the gauge, followed by the letters below for each type of metal in my studio. For example, 22 Cu is 22-gauge copper, or 16 AuR is 16-gauge rose gold. For gold, you must also designate the karat, so add a second set of numbers to specify that: 16 AuR-14K would be 14-karat rose gold, 16-gauge.

Al - Aluminum

Ag - Silver

Au - Gold, Y for yellow, R for rose, W for white

Cu - Copper

Ni - Nickel

Ti - Titanium

Alloys are a bit tricky, but because I use three popular base metals, I have developed this notation method: **BS** for brass, **BZ** for Bronze, **NG** for NuGold. This system works for me; however, you may develop one of your own.

Storing and Labeling Metal

It is important to have a system for storing metals in your workspace to avoid loss, damage, or confusion. One helpful tool to identify metal for storage is a permanent ink black marking pen such as a Sharpie. As soon as I return from a supplier with metal, the first thing I do is mark the gauge and the type of metal directly on the sheet in several places. I store sheet in zipper closure plastic bags and place them flat in a chest of drawers. I often store the invoice in the same bag. That way, I have an idea of how much that metal cost me no matter when I decide to use it.

A good system for metal storage is an index card noting the vendor, price paid, date, and the original size/weight, type and form of each piece of metal. Store metal in plastic or paper envelopes to prevent scratches and tarnish.

JEWELRY STONES

GEMSTONES are primarily minerals, although a few types of gems are formed from other organic materials. Gemstones used for jewelry are often colorful, beautiful, and inspiring, and many have a long-held appeal in terms of value and status. The decision to use a stone in a piece of jewelry is usually made at the design phase. Many jewelry makers begin their work with a splendid or special stone and work to create the metal fittings around it.

However, some jewelry makers cut their own stones as well as do the metalwork, which allows them to develop the piece in an organic way, making adjustments to either metal or stone at any point during creation. Of the more than 3,000 known minerals, only about 50 are regarded as gemstones. Of those 50, the rarest, and therefore most expensive, stones are traditionally used in the majority of commercially manufactured jewelry. These include diamonds, rubies, sapphires, and emeralds. Artisan jewelry designs often feature stones that are less rare, but no less beautiful.

Gemstone rough

Minerals are natural materials that are mined and collected for many purposes. The minerals in cut or uncut gemstones share many qualities, including hardness, durability, appealing color, luster, reflectivity, transparency, inclusions, and other optical properties. Most often, a stone's transparency is the main determinant for how it is cut. Opaque stones, sometimes called semiprecious gems, are typically cut into cabochons, while transparent stones are typically cut into faceted gems. However, many gems are cut in unexpected or nontraditional forms, particularly for unique works of artisan jewelry.

A sampling of gemstones that are less rare, but still beautiful options for your jewelry making.

Gemstone rough to faceted

Uncut amethyst

Faceted

Cabochon

Polished freeform slab with natural crystal profile

Physical properties of gemstones

Hardness is probably the most important quality for a durable gemstone. For jewelry pieces made to be worn every day, a stone that resists scratching, chipping, and wear and tear is the most suitable. The Mohs scale of mineral hardness is a common way to classify stones in their relative order of durability. Each stone on the scale will mark or scratch the surface of the ones lower than it, but not the ones higher than it.

Cleavage and fracture are somewhat predictable ways a gemstone or crystal will break. Cleavage planes are based on the atomic structure of a stone and are the areas of weakest bonding within a stone. They are usually parallel, diagonal, or perpendicular to the faces of the crystal. Fractures are broken surfaces that are not related to the atomic structure of the stone and are typically uneven.

OPTICAL PROPERTIES of a gemstone are based on the way light reflects off the surface of a stone, in addition to the way light passes through it. Gemstone color is the result of many factors, including the chemical composition or base color of the stone, plus the effects of impurities or trace elements. For example, transparent quartz can be clear, purple, yellow, pink, green, milky, brown or smoky, but it is all quartz.

Mohs Scale of Mineral Hardness
[1 = softest; 10 = hardest]

1. Talc
2. Gypsum
3. Calcite
4. Fluorite
5. Apatite
6. Orthoclase
7. Quartz
8. Topaz
9. Corundum
10. Diamond

Faceted Stone Shapes

RECTANGLE
Scissor-cut
41 Facets

CUSHION
Step-cut
49 Facets

OCTAGON
Eight-cut
17 Facets

OVAL
Split Mains
81 Facets

ROUND
Standard Brilliant
57 Facets

SQUARE
Brilliant
65 Facets

HEART
69 Facets

PENDELOQUE OR PEAR
Step-cut
57 Facets

CUT STONES come in two common styles: cabochon or faceted. Some cut stones are also carved into **cameos**, where the carving is raised above the main surface, or **intaglios**, where a carving is incised or engraved into the rear surface of a transparent stone, or down into the top surface of an opaque one.

TUMBLED STONES are those stones that are left in their natural crystal form and simply polished by tumbling.

CABOCHONS offer a simple way to cut a stone using a variety of mechanical or hand-grinding equipment. The art of creating cut stones is called **lapidary**, and it is an old and very popular art form on its own. Cabochon gemstones traditionally feature a highly polished and domed surface, with a polished or unpolished flat back. Cabochons are most often bezel set, but can also be set in tension, prong, tabbed, or other types of mounts or settings.

FACETED STONES are most often transparent and are cut to give them a series of measured, flat surfaces called **facets**. Facets both reflect light and absorb light and, in a traditional cut, their placement is mathematically determined based on the optical properties of the stone. The documented system for the calculated cutting of a faceted stone is called a **facet design**, and any given basic shape can be faceted in limitless ways. Faceted transparent stones are usually set to allow light to pass through them for maximum sparkle. Typical settings for such stones include prongs, open-back bezels, channels, tube sets, basket, and crown settings and mounts.

Tumbled gemstones

Malachite

Chrysocolla

Red tiger's eye

Snowflake obsidian

Dalmatian jasper

Brown tiger's eye

Cabochon gemstones

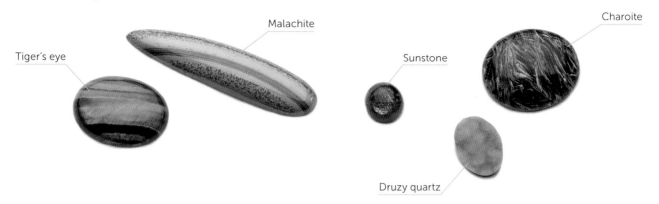

Tiger's eye

Malachite

Sunstone

Charoite

Druzy quartz

Cameos and intaglios

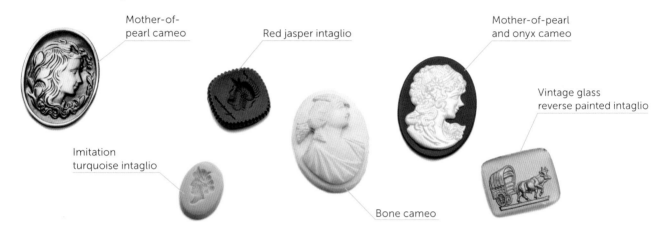

Mother-of-pearl cameo

Red jasper intaglio

Mother-of-pearl and onyx cameo

Vintage glass reverse painted intaglio

Imitation turquoise intaglio

Bone cameo

Faceted gemstones

Trilliant-cut rutilated quartz

Fancy round-cut citrine

Square-cut tourmalinated quartz

Concave-cut round smoky quartz

Oval-cut blue topaz

Rectangle-cut treated "Mystic" topaz

Colors of Gemstones

WHITE: Milky quartz, moonstone, howlite, agate, nephrite, mother-of-pearl

CLEAR: Albite, diamond, quartz, scheelite, moonstone, zircon, sapphire, topaz

PINK: Kunzite, rose quartz, thulite, morganite, rhodochrosite, rhodonite, spinel, tourmaline

RED: Ruby, pyrope, almandine, spinel, jasper, rubellite, agate, garnet, coral

YELLOW: Citrine, prehnite, sphalerite, heliodor, amber, scheelite, diamond, fluorite, sapphire, zircon, mustard jasper

ORANGE: Sapphire, opal, sard, carnelian, spessartine, agate, coral, sunstone

BROWN: Epidote, chrysoberyl, aragonite, smoky quartz, hypersthene, dravite, hessionite, diamond, spessartine, sphalerite, agate, tiger's eye

GREEN: Crysocolla, peridot, emerald, malachite, moldavite, beryl, diopside, jade, serpentine, bloodstone, agate, tourmaline, aventurine, nephrite, prehnite, sapphire, tourmaline, hiddenite, garnet, apatite, fluorite

BLUE: Indicolite, turquoise, lapis lazuli, aquamarine, azurite, dumortierite, kyanite, sapphire, zircon, topaz, fluorite, benitoite, dumortierite, spinel, apatite, diamond

BLACK: Hematite, diamond, schorl, jet, obsidian, garnet, diopside, agate

PURPLE: Purpurite, topaz, charoite

Colored gemstones

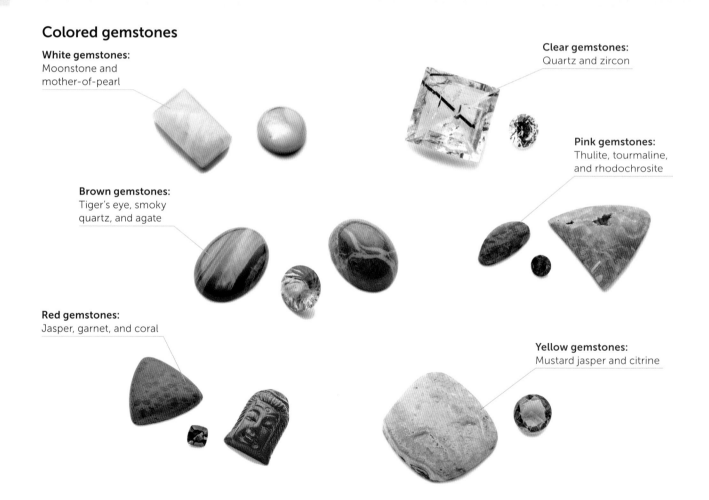

White gemstones:
Moonstone and mother-of-pearl

Clear gemstones:
Quartz and zircon

Pink gemstones:
Thulite, tourmaline, and rhodochrosite

Brown gemstones:
Tiger's eye, smoky quartz, and agate

Red gemstones:
Jasper, garnet, and coral

Yellow gemstones:
Mustard jasper and citrine

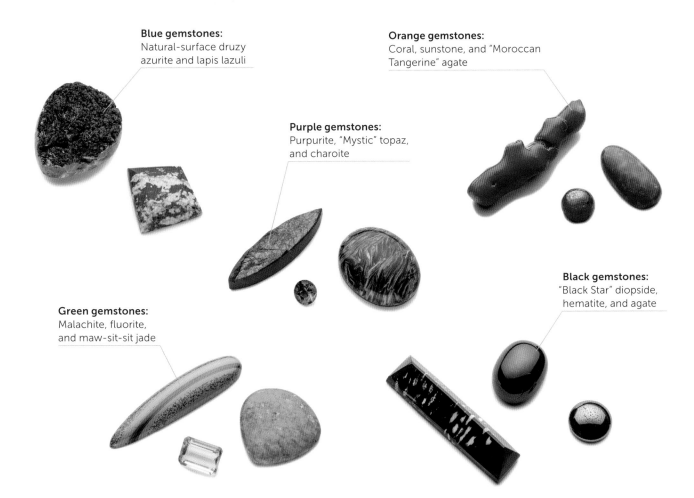

Blue gemstones:
Natural-surface druzy azurite and lapis lazuli

Orange gemstones:
Coral, sunstone, and "Moroccan Tangerine" agate

Purple gemstones:
Purpurite, "Mystic" topaz, and charoite

Black gemstones:
"Black Star" diopside, hematite, and agate

Green gemstones:
Malachite, fluorite, and maw-sit-sit jade

OTHER JEWELRY MATERIALS

In addition to metal and stone, there are hundreds of other materials suitable for making jewelry. Unlike precious metal and rare gemstones, many of these materials are inexpensive and widely available. Glass; plastics and polymers; leather; paper; fabric; ceramic; fibers; natural materials such as shell, seeds, or wood; recycled objects; and many others are all ripe for the using in artisan jewelry.

Anything can be used as a raw material in jewelry work—as long as wearability and durability are considered in the creation of the object. Perhaps the most important property in a well-made and well-designed piece of jewelry is durability. If the chosen material will withstand daily wear and the method used to construct the work is sturdy and secure, chances are it will be a successful work of jewelry art. Like jewelry metals, most of these alternate materials offer two choices for the artist: the option to purchase manufactured components or the option to purchase raw materials and to custom-build elements as desired.

PLASTICS include resin, PVC, acrylic, and vintage plastics such as Bakelite, celluloid, and others. Many premade forms are available—sheet, rod, tubes, discs, balls, and other shapes—in addition to plastics in liquid form that can be mixed and cast in molds. Polymer clay is a very popular raw material and easy to find in craft stores. Resins and epoxies can be colored and cast in thousands of ways and the options for using them are virtually limitless. In general, plastics are very durable, versatile materials.

Modern **plastics** include polymer clay, acrylic, vinyl, resin, Plexiglas, and PVC. Many vintage plastics such as Bakelite, celluloid, Lucite, and bonded polymers provide inspiring raw materials for jewelry making.

Plastics

Glass

GLASS includes enamel, beads, cabochons, sheet, tube, discs, marbles, and hundreds of other manufactured forms. It comes in a wide variety of colors and is typically inexpensive, but it breaks easily. **Glass** can be fused, slumped, made into beads, ground, cut, pierced, etched, sandblasted, drilled, and glued. For flamework, glass rod is used, allowing the jewelry artist to create specific components in myriad forms. Also, the art of enameling is often a specialist discipline in jewelry work.

Glass for jewelry use takes many forms: rod for flamework, glass beads and components, modern and vintage cabochons, and recycled window glass are all colorful and often inexpensive sources of raw materials.

LEATHER and **FIBERS** are common jewelry materials and have great potential for adding color and surface texture in jewelry work. Leather forms include skins, bands, lacing, and cord, while fibers range from natural undyed fleece to neon-bright synthetic cords. Every natural or synthetic fiber or material can be made into a jewelry material using any of the fiber arts disciplines: weaving, knitting, sewing, tatting, netting, crochet, knotting, and more.

Leathers, skins, and cords can be used in fittings, in connection methods, or as mounting vehicles for pendants and other forms of jewelry.

Fibers, fleece, and fabric can be combined with metalwork, or can be used alone to create jewelry featuring sewing, weaving, or any number of needle arts.

Leather

Fibers

CERAMIC is another material that offers limitless variety for jewelry work. Like glass, it can break, though not as easily. Ceramic components include beads, pendants, discs, tubes, cabochons, tiles, and many others. Porcelain, terra cotta, raku, glazed or natural, brightly colored, shiny or matte are just a few options. Clay is another raw material that allows the jewelry artisan to use a multidisciplinary approach to design: it can be hand-built, cast, molded, cut, sandblasted, glazed, drilled, and glued as well.

Ceramics are durable and colorful: beads, cabochons or hand-built elements such as pendants or tiles, and broken shards of vintage or new china often feature beautiful and inspiring patterns, designs, and colors for unique jewelry materials.

PAPER and WOOD are becoming very popular materials in contemporary jewelry and are light, durable, and readily available. Hundreds of paper choices allow the jewelry-making artist to experiment with color, surface texture, folds, layering and calligraphy, drawing, or painting. Making handmade paper is an example of how an artist can begin with the raw materials and custom-build components. Wood can be sawn, stained, painted, carved, molded, burned, milled, and textured, much like paper, and is easily combined with other materials.

Wood is a subtle but durable jewelry material that can be carved, cut, dyed, painted, or stained.

Ceramics

Wood

NATURAL and **FOUND OBJECTS** are fantastic materials to ignite the imagination. Twigs, seeds, small rocks, feathers, shells, leaves, and other objects have been used in jewelry since the beginning of mankind. Many ethnic or tribal works feature these materials, which are joined by ingenious methods. Organics can be fragile: much thought should be given to their use so they remain intact through wear. Found objects include cast-off remnants of modern manufactured life as well—bottle caps, buttons, wire, metal, plastics, printed materials, books, containers, household goods, clothing, etc. With an open mind and inventive approach, you can use any inspiring object in jewelry work. One person's trash can indeed be another's treasure.

Handmade or **manufactured papers** and vintage ephemera have become quite popular for jewelry making, especially when used in combination with mixed-media work or with cold-connected pieces.

Natural and **organic found materials**, including shells, pebbles, twigs, and stones, can be fun to hunt for as well as use in jewelry work.

Found objects can also include a wide array of items such as buttons, trinkets, toys, mechanical parts, keys, and other remnants of the man-made world, which provide an unexpected and often amusing element in jewelry work.

Paper

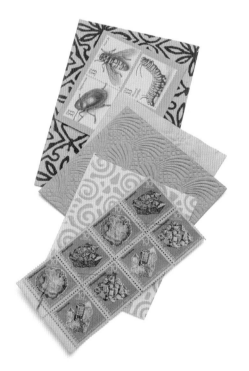

Natural and found objects

PART TWO:
Into the Workshop

Generally, artists are notorious hoarders of raw material and are not known for their organizational skills. That said, it is important to arrange your workspace in a way that is *safe, logical, and efficient for you.*

SHOP LAYOUT AND SAFETY

Every tool, material, and partially finished or finished object needs a space where it will be used *and* a space where it will be stored. For many jewelry makers, this is a stumbling point and often results in a disorganized workshop with mounds of materials and tools strewn on every available flat surface. If you find yourself having to move a jumbled mess of things constantly in order to work, examine your storage solutions and make the time to better arrange your shop with an eye to efficiency and logic. It is worth spending time to organize well in the beginning, since you will save time over the long run by not having to hunt for tools or materials because you don't know where they are.

There seems to be a never-ending series of conflicting needs in most jewelry studios, making an efficient layout in anything other than a designated studio difficult, but not impossible. Steel tools must be used dry, while lapidary equipment makes a wet mess. The pickling area needs to be near the torch, but also near a sink and an outlet. You may or may not wish to solder at your bench: either way, you will need a fireproof surface and ventilation. Torch tanks and lines must be located in a secure and sturdy area that is accessible, but protected. Dust and grime are inevitable when polishing and sanding, but metal must be pristine clean when soldering.

For many artists, creating a functional studio is as much an in-progress work of art as the works created within one. Rather than map out a way for you to arrange your particular workspace, I encourage you to use the following guidelines to either plan a new space or modify the one you've got. Think about what you would like to do, what your particular use zones and storage needs are, and set up your space accordingly. Finally, never forget safety: it should always be the forethought that guides you when you touch the tool you intend to use next.

Use zones

In a jewelry studio, tools and materials are used in three or more general regions: a bench or worktable, specialized tool regions (either wet or dry), and the soldering area. Think carefully about your shop and the work you want to make. How to arrange your shop and storage depends on the work you do and your personality, so make some detailed notes on how you work, how often you perform specific tasks, and what your future needs might be. Once you have a priority list, start sketching use zones and keep in mind that some zones can be multifunctional.

Ideally, use zones should be situated in a work triangle, with good lighting, proper ventilation and plumbing if needed, and seating or standing areas at each one. *The golden rule of use zones is this: if they are not being used, they should be free of tools and materials.* In my shop, I clear the work surfaces and put everything away at the end of a work session. A work session can last anywhere from an hour to a month—by definition, it is the time it takes to complete the object I am making during that session. If I have to interrupt a work session, I store the unfinished work and materials in a job box with any related notes, receipts, or sketches. It takes discipline to do this consistently, but it is important to return your tools to the place where they are stored. The time you save by developing this habit will allow you to make more jewelry, which is what every jewelry maker desires.

Storage zones

Storage is a complex issue for jewelry makers, because the things we need to store and use range from tiny gemstones to hefty 100-pound anvils. *The golden rule of storage is very easy: objects should first be grouped by what they are and what they do.* After that, how you store them is based on your personal preferences.

For a new space, use your planning notes to arrange the storage zones. If you are digging out of an existing work area that hasn't been efficient, this can be daunting. Start with a macro-sort: gather all like objects and take an inventory. Then do a micro-sort of those same objects based on your work personality. Look for storage containers, shelving, and cabinetry that will contain the objects you need to store but that require the least possible space. And don't forget to allow for expansion, especially for most-used categories of tools, materials, and reference materials. Storage zones are generally dry and need not be near their associated use zone, except in the case of tools. Tools are best stored adjacent to the use zone where they will be used.

Work personality

Keep your personality in mind as you create your workspace. Artists are visual people: often seeing the materials they are going to use is what triggers the creative act. Choose storage with this in mind. For example, colorful stones or beads can be stored in many ways—in lidded boxes, in drawers, in stacked transparent containers, in jars on shelves, or on strands hanging from pegboard. All of those storage methods are efficient. But for an artist who needs to touch, see, and compare color for inspiration, perhaps hanks of beads hung on a pegboard is a better solution than hiding them in lidded boxes.

Safety

The most important tools are not the ones for which you are trying to find a perfect storage solution: they are your hands, ears, eyes, and brain. Making jewelry is not inherently dangerous. However, tools, chemicals, and metal can injure you if you fail to take the proper safety precautions. You will inevitably get bruised, burned, and cut over time. What you want to do is reduce the number of times that happens and minimize the extent of any injuries. Here are ten non-negotiable rules for working safe:

1. **Safety glasses** are a must when drilling, cutting, mixing, striking, sanding, abrading, polishing, etc. Please protect your eyes in any situation where there is the potential for flying metal, liquid, dust, particulates, or a broken tool.

2. **Ventilation** is imperative when soldering, firing, annealing, enameling, heating pitch, or using resin, patina solutions, or other chemicals. Install a ventilation hood if possible. Until you do, use a fan, open a window, and wear appropriate masks or respirators when soldering or being exposed to chemicals or particulates.

3. Wear **gloves** when mixing or using chemicals, but never at the buffing wheel. Also, wear heavy work gloves to protect your hands when cutting metal with tin snips.

4. If you intend to hammer or drill metal for prolonged periods, use **hearing protection**.

5. **Flameproof surfaces** are necessary when soldering, annealing, or removing fired objects from a kiln.

6. Keep a **first-aid kit** and a **fire extinguisher** handy and visible in the shop.

7. Wear **natural fiber clothing** when working with fire to prevent

Wearing a work apron and safety goggles is a good habit and will help protect two of your most important jewelry-making tools: you and your eyes.

severe secondary burns from melting synthetic fibers in the event of a spark.

8. When you are working, tie back long hair; wear snug-fitting clothing, short sleeves, shoes that cover your feet, and a protective apron; and wear no jewelry.

9. **Grounded electrical outlets and GFI circuits** in wet zones are essential for a well-powered studio. Minimize the number of extension cords you use and hire a professional electrician to wire your shop.

10. Read and follow all **manufacturer's directions** before using a tool or machine for the first time. If you are unsure of any process or how to use a tool, seek help from an experienced teacher before attempting a new technique or using an unfamiliar material. *When in doubt, don't proceed.*

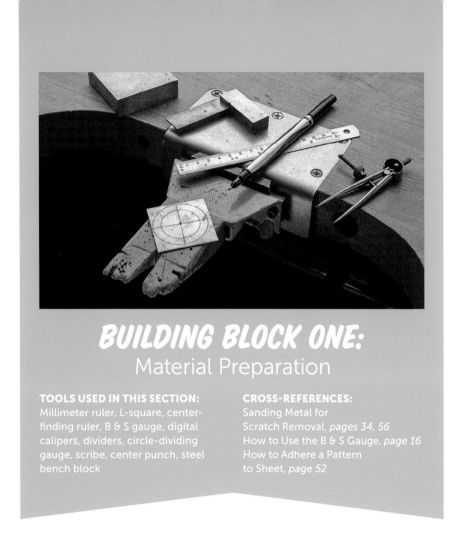

BUILDING BLOCK ONE:
Material Preparation

TOOLS USED IN THIS SECTION:
Millimeter ruler, L-square, center-finding ruler, B & S gauge, digital calipers, dividers, circle-dividing gauge, scribe, center punch, steel bench block

CROSS-REFERENCES:
Sanding Metal for Scratch Removal, *pages 34, 56*
How to Use the B & S Gauge, *page 16*
How to Adhere a Pattern to Sheet, *page 52*

Among studio jewelers, there is a popular maxim: *Well begun is half done.* Truer words were never spoken. To realize a creative work from an idea requires sustained focus and effort.

Mistakes can be costly when precious metal and expensive stone are involved. Successful work depends on careful preparation. Every jewelry object is initiated by an idea. After that, some artists plan the **design** and **layout** through model-making, sketching, and/or drawing. Next begins the gathering of the raw materials and tools. Many artists also rehearse the **fabrication** steps in their heads hundreds of times in order to know intimately how they will make the object. If necessary, they will conduct physical tests of unfamiliar techniques.

This process can take moments or months, depending on the complexity of the work and the skill of the maker.

One of the most important tools in a studio jeweler's arsenal cannot be purchased in any store: *patience.* It is a skill that develops through disciplined practice, the importance of which cannot be overstated. Physical dexterity and patience must evolve at the same rate. Once an artist accepts the premise that careful practice with the tools should be part of every workday, the door to beautiful and well-crafted works opens.

Measuring tools

It is tempting to begin making jewelry by just leaping in and experimenting with tools, metal, and pretty stones, but this approach can be costly in the long run. It is difficult but important to know just how much metal is needed for a project and how to use it economically. I tell my students to pretend that every piece of metal is expensive platinum and to cut it out accordingly. And, there is no place for vanity in the jewelry studio, so use whatever vision aids are needed for accurate measuring.

A **MILLIMETER RULER** is used during virtually every work session. Choose a well-made, tempered steel rule, with inches, millimeters, and a conversion chart on the back. Choose an etched ruler over a printed one, because printed text rubs off over time.

An **L-SQUARE** is a tool that will help you achieve precise 90° angle corners. Choose a 4-inch steel square if possible and try not to drop it since that will cause it to go out of alignment or bend. Some models have detachable feet, which allow them to stand erect on your work surface.

A **CENTER-FINDING RULER** is a handy tool, but not essential. Use it for symmetrical layout and accurate measurements from a center point.

A **B & S GAUGE** (also known as the American Wire Gauge/AWG) is the most critical tool to own for determining the thickness of sheet and wire. The "American Standard" system of measure differs from the "British Standard," so choose the tool for your region accordingly. Well-made gauges have tolerances of less than one 100th of a millimeter and are marked with gauge size on one side and decimal measure on the reverse.

DIGITAL CALIPERS eliminate the confusion and calculation of the old-fashioned sliding vernier caliper. On well-made calipers, a digital readout is displayed on the face of the tool; both the **inner diameter (ID)** and **outer diameter (OD)** can be measured accurately.

Measuring tools

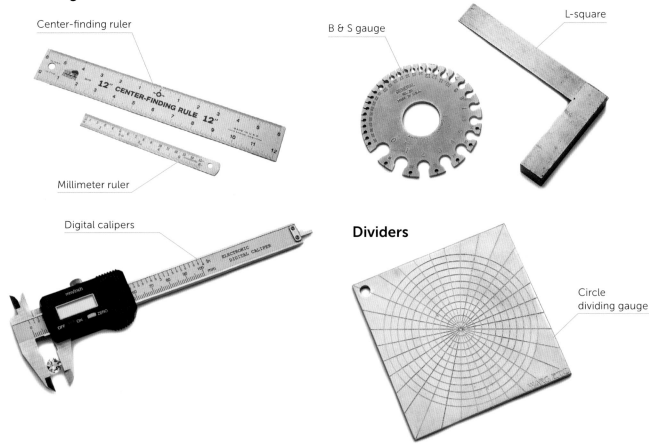

Center-finding ruler

Millimeter ruler

B & S gauge

L-square

Digital calipers

Dividers

Circle dividing gauge

DIVIDERS are one of the most versatile tools in the shop and are used for a wide variety of measuring and layout tasks. Shop for a hardened-steel set with a durable spring—this tool is deceptively simple, and a quality version can be expensive, but will last a lifetime.

Although the CIRCLE-DIVIDING GAUGE is one of the most difficult tools to locate and purchase, it is invaluable for the way it makes short work of marking equal divisions around a circle.

Layout tools

Several additional tools are essential for good layout, patternmaking and transfer, and to prepare saw-pierced or fretwork jewelry designs. It is helpful to have a clean, well-lit area to design and lay out with metal. A white surface makes seeing the work easier. Have a supply of paper, marking pens, tracing paper, drafting or masking tape, and thin cardboard on hand for making patterns and models.

A sharp SCRIBE can be used to incise cutting or fold lines on metal sheet. A scribed line is much thinner than a drawn one and will not rub off during sawing. Take care not to scribe too deeply or the surface of the metal can be damaged and will require sanding to remove the layout lines. When not in use, the scribe point should be sunk into cork or a kneaded eraser to prevent it from dulling—or injuring you.

Manual or automatic CENTER PUNCHES are used to make a small divot or dimple in the metal surface. The divot serves as a pilot hole for drilling or burring and aids precise hole placement.

A STEEL BENCH BLOCK is invaluable as a work surface when punching or stamping sheet metal because it prevents dents from forming when a tool is struck with a hammer or mallet. These are available in many sizes. In my shop, I reserve one side of the block for punching, marking it with a dot of red lacquer nail polish to indicate "punch-only" use. The other side is kept smooth and clear of dings and dents for hammer texturing because any marks in the steel will transfer to the jewelry metal whether intended or not.

Dividers (con't.)

Layout tools

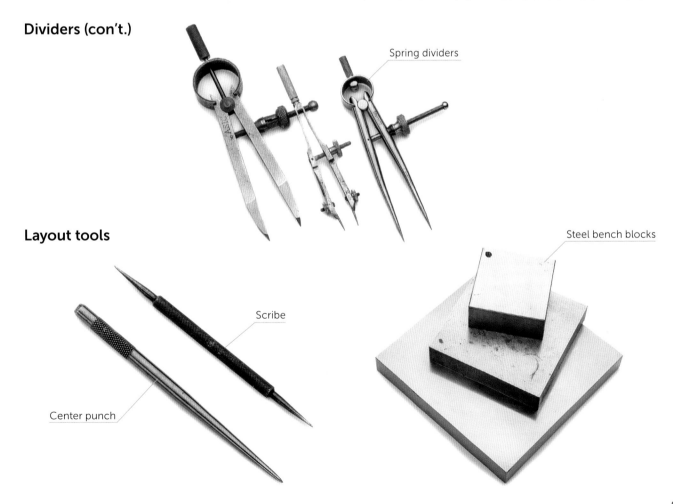

Spring dividers

Steel bench blocks

Scribe

Center punch

Universal Gauge Chart

B & S Gauge	Millimeters	Inches Decimal	Inches Fraction	Drill Bit Size	Blade Size
0	8.5	.325	21/64		
1	7.34	.289	9/32		
2	6.52	.257	1/4		
3	5.81	.229	7/32	1	
4	5.18	.204	13/64	6	
5	4.62	.182	3/16	15	
6	4.11	.162	5/32	20	
7	3.66	.144	9/64	27	
8	3.25	.128	1/8	30	
9	2.90	.114			
10	2.59	.102		38	
11	2.31	.091	3/32	43	
12	2.06	.081	5/64	45	8
13	1.83	.072		50	7
14	1.63	.064	1/16	51	6
15	1.45	.057		52	
16	1.30	.051		54	5 to 3
17	1.14	.045	3/64	55	4 to 2
18	1.02	.040		56	3 to 1
19	0.914	.036		60	1 to 1/0
20	0.812	.032	1/32	65	1/0 to 2/0
21	0.711	.028		67	2/0 to 3/0
22	0.635	.025		70	4/0
23	0.558	.022		71	5/0
24	0.508	.020		74	6/0
25	0.457	.018		75	7/0
26	0.406	.016	1/64	77	8/0
28	0.304	.012		79	
29	0.279	.011		80	
30	0.354	.010			

Cleaning metal

When laying out a design, it is important to start with a blemish- and scratch-free sheet of metal that is clear of grease, fingerprints, and oils. Scrub the sheet just before laying it out to prevent tarnish from forming over time. Several products work well for metal: have a well-labeled stock of these near the sink—nondetergent dish liquid such as Ivory, pumice powder, nondetergent abrasive cleanser, baking soda, coarse salt, and alcohol. *(Fig. 1)*

I find it helpful to work on a terra-cotta flat tile to prevent the metal from warping as I scrub it with a soft brass brush or 3M Scotch-Brite pad. Water will sheet off of clean metal in an unbroken stream. If there are gaps or voids in the water when the metal is rinsed clean, grease, oil, or dirt remains on the surface and the metal must be scrubbed again. *(Figs. 2 & 3)*

I keep a supply of white cotton rags, paper towels, scrub brushes, and old toothbrushes handy as well. Dedicated plastic food containers and assorted Pyrex dishes are also good to have on hand for soaking metal in chemicals or solvents. *Do not ever use these containers to hold food.*

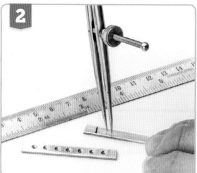

Three ways to use dividers

Good-quality dividers will create a very accurate scribed line on metal sheet. Use them to create even borders or cutting lines that are parallel to the edges of any shape—even curved ones. Dividers can be used to transfer a series of evenly spaced measurements across a sheet of metal or around a 3-D object. Pivot the dividers from point to point in a series of arcs, making a gentle scribe mark at each step of the walk.

1. Choose a measurement and line up the legs of the dividers within the etched lines of the millimeter gauge. Transfer the measure to the sheet. *(Fig. 1)*

2. "Walk" a preset measure across or around a component to make equal divisions of that measurement. Place the dividers, leave one leg in position, and pivot around it to make the next mark. Repeat as many times as needed. *(Figs. 2 & 3)*

3. To scribe a line parallel to a cut edge, set a measurement, then hang one leg of the divider over the edge and lightly trace the perimeter of the sawn shape. *(Fig. 4)*

How to use a center punch

It is important to create a divot or pilot hole in metal sheet prior to drilling it to allow maximum accuracy. An unpunched metal surface will cause the drill bit to skip or slide over the surface, potentially breaking the bit or creating an off-center hole.

4. Mark with a dot where a hole is required. Position the point of the punch on the dot. *(Fig. 5)*

5. Strike the punch once to create a shallow divot in the sheet. Drill the hole with a small drill bit and insert the saw blade to saw out the opening. Or use progressively larger bits to create a round, drilled hole. *(Fig. 6)*

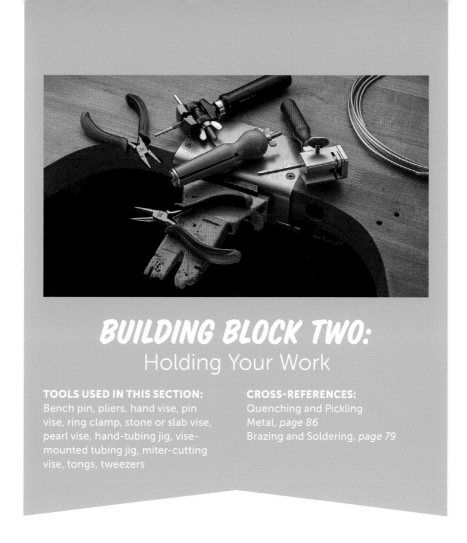

BUILDING BLOCK TWO:
Holding Your Work

TOOLS USED IN THIS SECTION:
Bench pin, pliers, hand vise, pin vise, ring clamp, stone or slab vise, pearl vise, hand-tubing jig, vise-mounted tubing jig, miter-cutting vise, tongs, tweezers

CROSS-REFERENCES:
Quenching and Pickling Metal, *page 86*
Brazing and Soldering, *page 79*

If I had a dollar for every minute I spent in the studio trying to figure out the best way to hold onto something while I worked on it, I would be a very wealthy person.

Half of the problem-solving required to make jewelry is typically related to holding tiny things in position as you saw, file, manipulate, rivet, solder, grind, polish, or set. For every category of fabrication, there is a huge array of specialized holding and gripping tools on the market. Having a variety of these tools at your bench makes fabrication easier: there is nothing more satisfying than having exactly the right one at your fingertips just when you need it. Clamps, grips, and supports make working more efficient, so it is wise to invest in several of the general-duty ones, then add the specialty tools as your work requires.

The bench pin

The humble bench pin is the most used tool in the jewelry shop. All artists customize the pin as they work—by intentionally or accidentally cutting into it or by modifying the profile of the pin as they fabricate work. A bench pin is sculpted over time during the process of making work: the contours of each jeweler's bench pin are evidence of what they have made. Purchase a sturdy hardwood bench pin, as it will last many, many years. I never drill into mine, but some artists do not mind the resulting holes. The flat side of the pin is for saw-piercing and the angled side is for filing. Take the time to flip the pin as you work to ensure proper support of your work and tools. Many artists begin by using a portable pin attached to a table then later invest in a jeweler's bench.

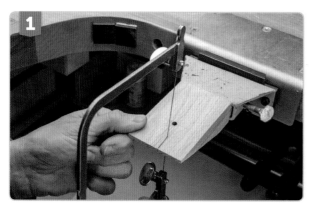

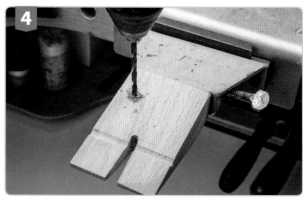

How to customize a stock bench pin

1. Cut a V-shaped slot in the pin. The V-slot will allow you to saw-pierce more efficiently and it is a useful place to park tools, fingers, or parts to steady them as you fabricate. Drill a pilot hole in the pin and then saw a V into it with a coarse saw blade. Sand any sharp edges as desired. Over time, the process of fabricating work will sand the sharp edges all by itself. *(Fig. 1)*

2. Use a wood rasp to create an angled ramp on the right fork of the pin for filing and steadying things. If you are left-handed, do this on the left fork of the pin. *(Fig. 2)*

3. Use a round, untapered wood rasp to create a perpendicular groove about ¼" (6 mm) from the back of the V-slot. The little half-pipe groove provides a good place to steady tubing, round wire, or bar stock while sawing. *(Fig. 3)*

4. Drill a ⅛" (3 mm) diameter hole all the way through the bench pin, somewhere at the back, to insert earring posts, pin stems, wire, or tubing vertically. This is a handy way to check filed or polished edges and to hold things. Use this area to set tiny stones into bezels. *(Fig. 4)*

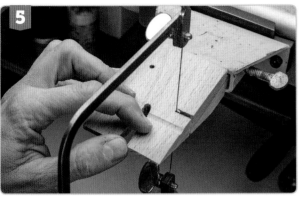

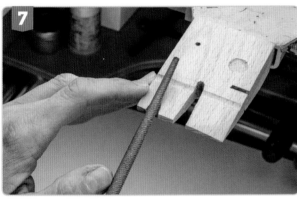

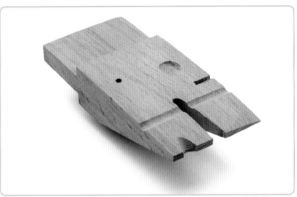

5. Cut a tweezer slot on the right (or left if you are left-handed) side of the pin. This is handy for spot-holding small parts in tweezers for very focused soldering at the bench. *(Fig. 5)*

6. Use a ball bur to create a "parking lot" for tiny stones or parts. *(Fig. 6)*

7. File a rounded notch on the left fork (if you are left-handed, notch the right fork) of the pin to brace parts for filing. Position it for your holding hand and angle it as needed. *(Fig. 7)*

Gripping tools

PLIERS are one of the largest categories of hand tools, and many artists have dozens of them. Think of pliers as mini fingers. Their jaws are designed to perform multiple functions—open, close, twist, pull, push, bend, grip, join, and compress. Pliers in four basic jaw designs should be purchased early on, as they are universally useful: **round-nose**, **flat-nose**, **chain-nose**, and **half-round**. Do not be tempted to scrimp on quality, because you will use the basic four almost every time you work.

HAND VISES include the ring clamp, pin vise, bead and pearl vises, and the hand vise. Each is versatile and invaluable for its designated task. I prefer a hardwood **ring clamp** with a wood wedge. Work can be held at either end during filing, sawing, grinding, or polishing. The **pin vise** grips wire very securely and works well for pin stems—particularly in tandem with a filed groove in the bench pin. The **hand vise** features pegs and a screw thread to clamp the jaws inward and to support oddly shaped work. For longevity, purchase vises with all-metal parts: plastic parts will wear out under the pressure of fabricating metal. **Stone** or **slab** and **pearl vises** are designed for holding stones and pearls securely during drilling.

JIGS hold sheet, tubing, or other stock during sawing. The **tube-cutting jig** prevents slippage, and many models feature a measurement rod so that many sections of same-size stock can be sawn. They are available in right- or left-handed models. Harder to find is a **vise-mounted tubing jig**, which works the same way. The **miter cutting vise** makes precise fabrication a pleasure. Sheet, rod, and tubing can be held and scribed or sawn at several angles: 45°, 60°, and 90°. Choose a hardened-steel model.

Pliers: *the basic four*

Chain-nose
Flat-nose
Round-nose
Half-round

Hand vises

Ring clamp

Hand vise with pegs

Pin vise

Slab- and stone-drilling vise

Pearl-drilling vise

Jigs

Tube-cutting jig

Miter cutting vise/jig for tube, rod, and sheet

Vise-mounted tube and rod-sawing jig

TONGS and TWEEZERS are essential in several places in the studio: the workbench, the sink, and the soldering station. At the bench, good **steel tweezers** with sturdy points are useful for picking up beads, stones, and small components. Some models include a sliding lock to grip an object like a stone, pearl, or small metal part securely without letting go. There are also specialty tweezers for gemstones.

At the sink or ultrasonic cleaning station, **plastic- or rubber-tipped tweezers** are useful for removing jewelry from chemical baths or hot water after steam cleaning. Bamboo or plastic tweezers are useful during **patination** because they are washable and will not contaminate or change the chemistry of a solution.

Keep several kinds of specialty tweezers at the soldering station: **cross-lock tweezers**, **curved straight-nose tweezers**, and **tweezers mounted in a "third-hand" device** to position objects during soldering. You will use these for ring shanks, placing solder, and moving hot parts during soldering.

COPPER TONGS are for **pickling** only. Never use steel tweezers near the pickle pot. In the acidic pickle bath, steel or iron initiates a chemical reaction that causes copper that has become suspended in the pickle to plate whatever metal is present in the batch as long as the steel or iron is present in the solution. Instead, move pieces in and out of the pickle bath with copper or plastic tongs. I never move work directly from soldering into the pickle pot. I prefer to quench hot work in clean water, then transfer pieces into the pickle after they have been quenched. This also allows me to inspect my work and re-solder as needed—sometimes pickle prevents good solder flow on a previously soldered seam. Copper tongs will become annealed and lose their spring if they are used during soldering, so do not use them anywhere except at the pickle pot.

Tongs and tweezers

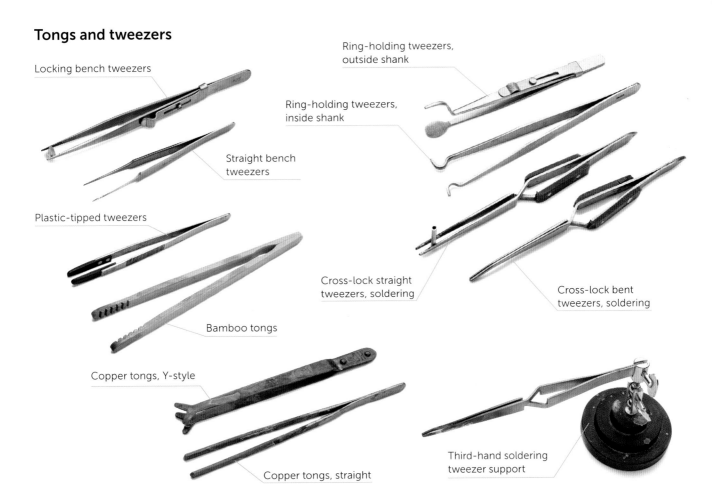

Locking bench tweezers

Ring-holding tweezers, outside shank

Ring-holding tweezers, inside shank

Straight bench tweezers

Plastic-tipped tweezers

Cross-lock straight tweezers, soldering

Cross-lock bent tweezers, soldering

Bamboo tongs

Copper tongs, Y-style

Copper tongs, straight

Third-hand soldering tweezer support

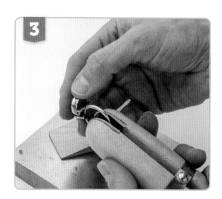

How to use a tube-cutting jig

Repetitive cuts are easy with a tube-cutting jig: just set the measurement, insert the tubing into the curved slot, and hold the thumb clamp firmly. Saw slowly and take care not to press too hard on the thumb clamp—otherwise, the saw blade might bind.

1. Set the jig to the desired length and insert the tubing into the slot with the cut edge positioned against the end bar. Hold the thumb clamp firmly against the tubing. *(Fig. 1)*

2. Insert an appropriately sized saw blade into the saw slot and carefully sever the tube. Take care not to allow the tubing to spin as you saw and do not apply excessive force to the blade. If you are cutting several sections to the same length, lift the clamp, slide the tubing to the end bar, and repeat. *(Fig. 2)*

How to use a ring clamp

A hardwood ring clamp is one of the most useful holding tools for the workshop. After inserting the ring or other part into the chosen jaw, give the wedge a sharp tap on a steel block to firmly grip the work in the leather pads of the tool opening.

1. Insert the ring shank or other piece into the clamp at the appropriate jaw—the tool is reversible—positioning it for the task you will perform. A clamp with leather pads prevents marring and also cushions the work. *(Fig. 3)*

2. Insert the wedge into the other jaw and tap it down on the work surface to grip the piece tightly. *(Fig. 4)*

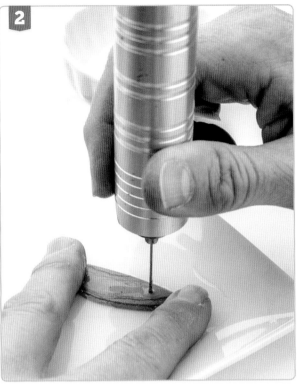

How to use pearl or stone vises

Drilling an undrilled pearl or enlarging the hole of a drilled one with a diamond drill bit should be done slowly. It is important to keep the pearl wet and to gradually enlarge the hole by increasing the diameter of the drill bit in steps. Drill all the way through the pearl using one size drill bit before stepping up to the next diameter.

Stone must also be drilled wet using diamond drill bits. I work in a shallow dish of water, dipping the drill tip often to keep it cool. The stone or the drill bit must never be allowed to dry out as you work.

1. **PEARL VISE.** Insert the pearl into the opening of the vise and tighten the knob. Use a small-diameter drill or bur to drill the pearl gently without overheating it. Work slowly and wet: do not try to drill too large a hole immediately. It is better to step up from a small, but well-drilled hole to the next diameter drill bit. *(Fig. 1)*

STONE VISE. Submersible and rustproof aluminum slab and bead vises are available specifically for drilling stone.

2. Stone must be drilled wet using diamond drill bits. Work in a shallow dish of water, dipping the tip of the drill in water to keep it cool. Take care not to allow the stone or the drill to dry out and clear any sludge from the hole as you drill. *(Fig. 2)*

Specialty Pliers

Pliers type	Jaw shape	Task
Looping	Round, untapered; also other shapes	Coils, loops, and jump rings
Confirming	Flat to flat; long sharp edges	Compressing folded metal
Parallel-action	Many varieties	Secure action; jaws close evenly across entire surface
Prong	Opening or closing	Setting or removing stones from pronged settings
Beading	Cupped tips	Create bead-shaped prong ends
Forming	Many varieties	Sturdy construction for bending thick stock or sheet
Ring/loop-closing	Slotted tips	Closing jump rings
Bow-opening	Slotted tips	Jaws open when handles are squeezed; for links and rings
Tube-holding	Slotted; stepped tips	To hold and saw thick wire or tubing
Ring-holding	Slotted; rounded	Similar to ring clamp; for inside shank work
Crimping	Grooved; stepped	Folding and flattening bead crimps
Split-ring	Tabbed tips	Opening split jump rings without marring
Hole-punching	Various shapes	Punching openings in thin sheet and flattened wire
Locking	Levered; tabbed	Hold work securely for polishing; soldering; cleaning

Specialty pliers

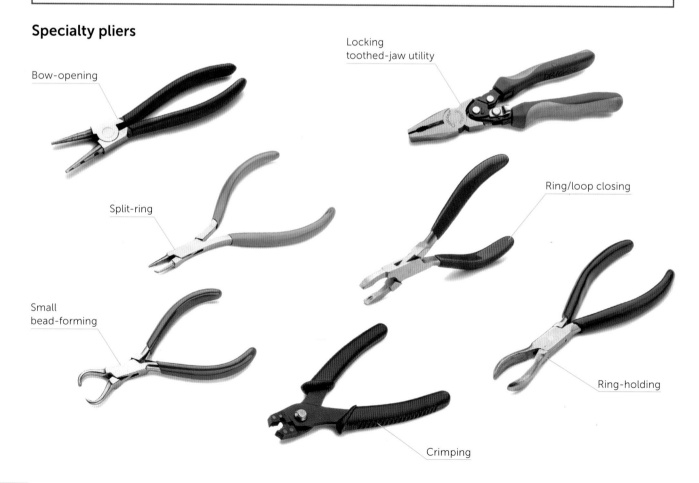

Bow-opening

Locking toothed-jaw utility

Split-ring

Ring/loop closing

Small bead-forming

Crimping

Ring-holding

Specialty pliers (con't.)

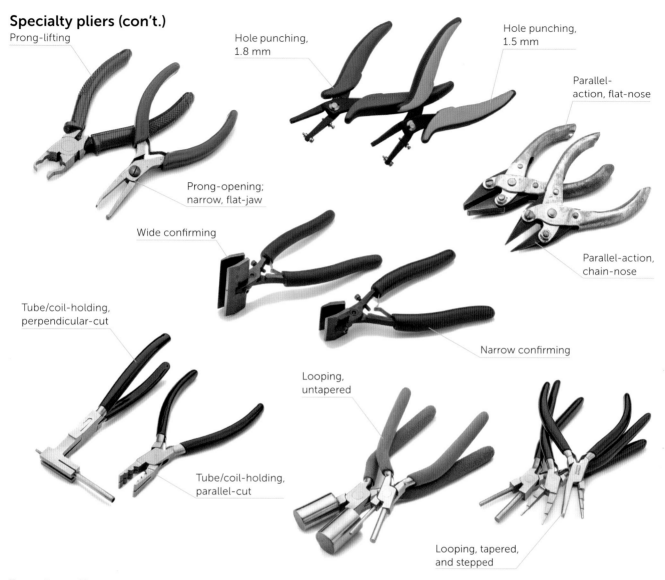

Prong-lifting

Hole punching, 1.8 mm

Hole punching, 1.5 mm

Parallel-action, flat-nose

Prong-opening; narrow, flat-jaw

Wide confirming

Parallel-action, chain-nose

Tube/coil-holding, perpendicular-cut

Narrow confirming

Looping, untapered

Tube/coil-holding, parallel-cut

Looping, tapered, and stepped

Forming pliers

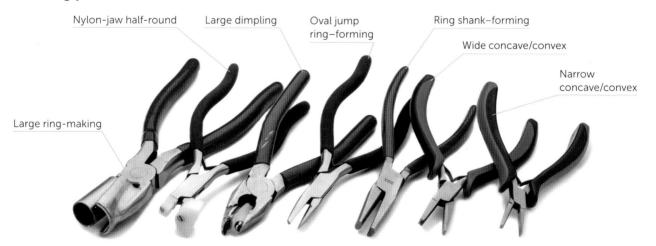

Nylon-jaw half-round

Large dimpling

Oval jump ring–forming

Ring shank–forming

Wide concave/convex

Narrow concave/convex

Large ring-making

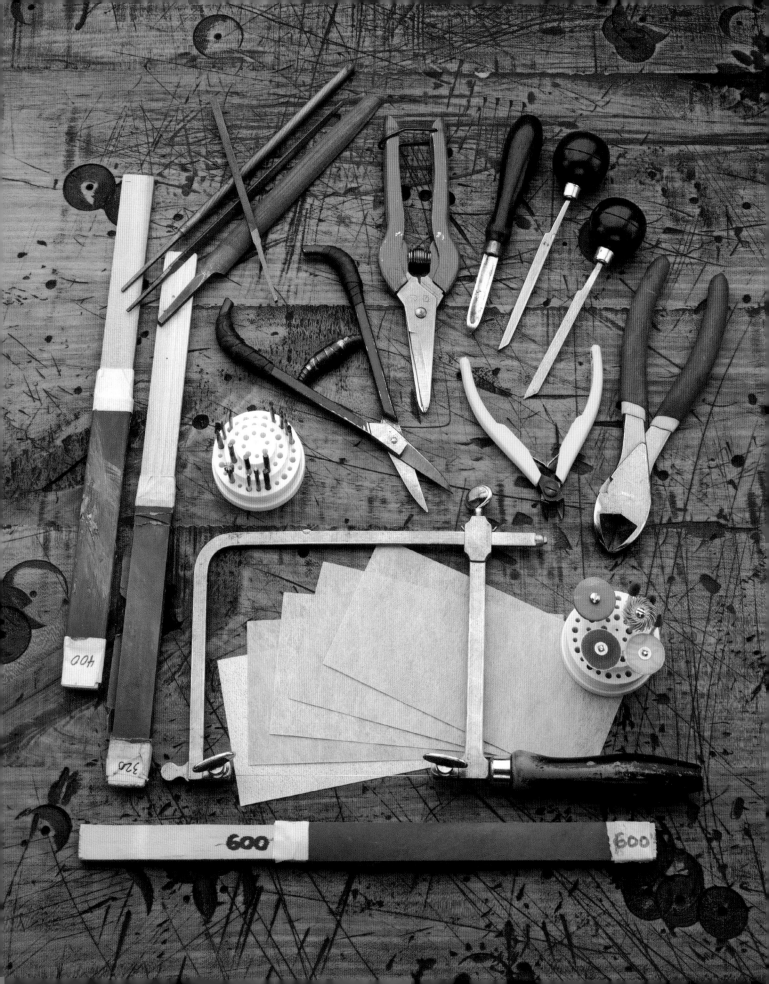

PART THREE:
At the Bench

BUILDING BLOCK THREE:
Piercing and Separating

TOOLS USED IN THIS SECTION:
Jeweler's saw and blades, triangle scraper, drill bits, gravers, snips, nippers, cutters, shears, circle- or disc-cutting punches, scissors

CROSS-REFERENCES:
Material Preparation, *page 31*
How to Use a Center Punch, *page 36*
Three Ways to Use Dividers, *page 36*
Universal Gauge Chart, *page 34*

Many tools are available for cutting metal sheet into smaller sections. Using snipping, notching, and cutting tools often results in an unsatisfactory cut because they can distort or mar the sheet along the edge due to the force needed to sever the metal.

They are best used for rough cutting. To achieve clean and undistorted cuts, sawing with a jeweler's saw is one of the most important metalworking skills to master. Expect to spend many hours perfecting your technique because there are many variables involved in doing it well: eye–hand coordination, technique, and tools all affect the outcome of saw-piercing or fretwork. Practice on many types of metal sheet in a variety of gauges using several different blade sizes—without an aim for producing anything more than a pile of metal scraps with cleanly and accurately sawn edges. Sawing is an essential jewelry-making skill that, when done well, will save time, effort, and material.

Cutting by compression

Chisels, metal snips, scissors, cutters, shears, and punches are all tools that create a cut edge by compressing the metal until it severs. For the hand tools, force is transferred to the sharp edges of the tool via hand strength: squeeze the tool closed and the metal thins and eventually severs where the sharp steel edges of the tool come together. The thicker the sheet, the more difficult it is to sever, and the more noticeable the edge distortion will be where the metal is severed. It is best to reserve

SNIPS and **CUTTERS** for rough cutting and for shaping thin-gauge metal. There will be no dust, shavings, or chips when these types of tools are used to cut metal. However, because of the force necessary to compress these tools, the waste metal portions curl into extremely sharp shards that may become airborne when they are severed. Always wear goggles and gloves for protection.

CHISELS and **DISC-** or **CIRCLE-CUTTING PUNCHES** compress metal, too, but the force needed to compress it requires the blow of a mallet, hammer or, in the case

of large circle die forms, a press to sever the metal. **CHISEL** cuts push the sharp edges of the severed area away from the tool; they must be filed and sanded to prevent discomfort when wearing. For best results when using a **HAND DISC-** or **CIRCLE-CUTTING PUNCH** within a **CUTTING DIE**, do not work in metal gauges thicker than 20 or in circle diameters larger than 1½" (3.8 cm). You risk damaging the tool with thicker sheet, and larger diameters are difficult to hold still during hammering. Do not use ferrous metals in a circle cutter: steel or iron will damage the cutting edge of the punch.

Compression cutting tools

Wire cutters, heavy gauge

Wire cutters, light gauge

Metal shears, French shop

All-purpose snips, titanium-jaw

Metal shears; heavy

Scissors, Joyce Chen brand

Sheet metal shears, tin snips

Sheet metal shears, straight

Cutting by gradual removal of material

Cutting an opening or groove by drilling, scraping, or engraving preserves the original thickness of metal sheet adjacent to the cut. Small amounts of metal are chipped, scraped, or flaked away by this group of tools. When a **TRIANGLE SCRAPER** or **GRAVER** is used, a small curl of metal called a **SWARF** will be raised from the surface of the sheet. This reduces the thickness of the metal where the tool was used: the swarf spirals up and away from the sharp edge of the tool as the metal is cut slowly. Drill bits work in the same fashion: their cutting edges spiral down the steel shaft of the bit to produce round openings. It is critical to protect the sharp cutting edges of these tools and to prevent the steel from rusting when they are not in use.

In saw-piercing, an opening, or **KERF**, will be created in the sheet the thickness of the saw blade. Small particles of metal, sometimes called **LEMEL**, will fall away from the kerf as the work progresses.

Compression cutting tools (con't.)

Cold chisels

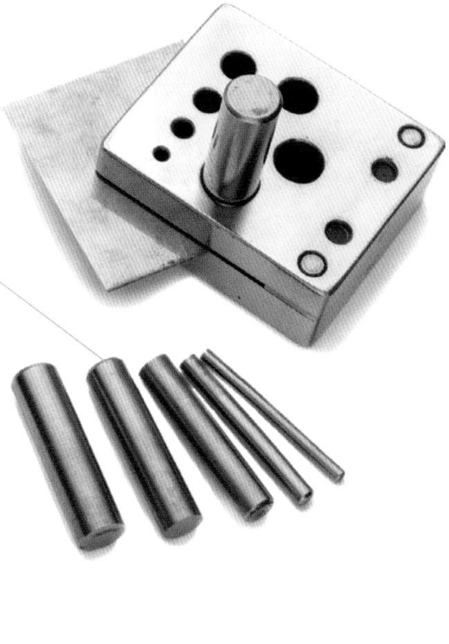

Material removal hand tools

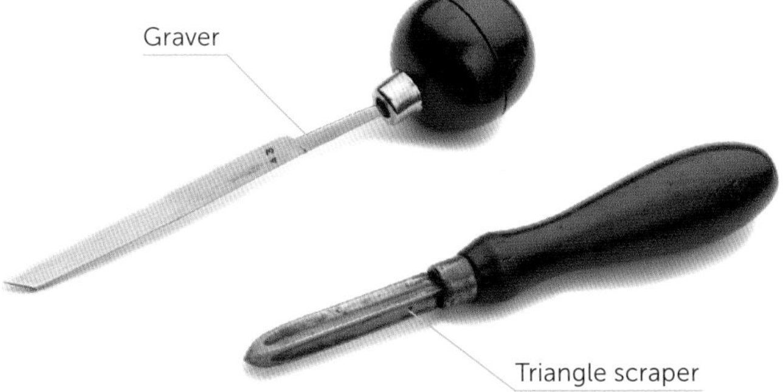

Graver

Triangle scraper

Disc cutter; die and punch set

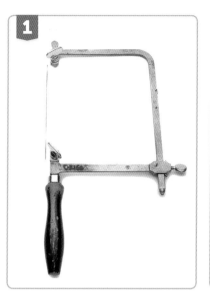

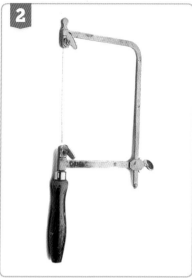

CHOOSING A SAW BLADE

- Intricate cuts call for fine blades.

- Curves are easier to cut with a fine blade.

- To drill a properly sized pilot hole for inside piercings, ensure the blade has enough clearance to move freely inside the drilled opening. To test the blade size for a particular drill bit, insert the saw blade in a drill gauge to measure.

- A blade should have a minimum of 3 teeth contacting the metal during sawing. If too few teeth contact the metal, the motion of the saw will be choppy and jumpy. Too many teeth may cause the blade to break. To compare, hold the blade spine against the metal sheet and examine them both from the side to see if the metal is 3-teeth deep.

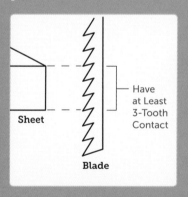

Sheet

Have at Least 3-Tooth Contact

Blade

The jeweler's saw: threading the blade and sawing

This simple tool is one of the most important in the craft of jewelry making. Sawing is a technique that takes committed practice to master, and it is important to learn how to proceed when multiple factors influence the outcome: metal type and gauge, blade size, type of cut, and level of experience of the jewelry maker.

Saw frames are engineered to hold the blade under tension. To create tension, a series of thumbscrews, pads, and washers allow minute adjustments to the frame depth, length, and the amount of pull on the blade. Here is how to thread the blade into the frame properly:

1. Choose a blade and examine the teeth. Ensure they face the outside of the saw frame and angle down, like a child's drawing of a Christmas tree. Hold the blade next to the frame for a visual comparison. Roughly, the frame should be set so it is slightly taller—about ½" (1.3 cm)—than the total length of the blade. *(Fig. 1)*

2. Insert the top of the blade between the frame and the pad, with the teeth facing out and down. The blade spine should remain parallel to the back bar of the saw frame, and the very top of the blade will touch the top of the opening at the set screw. Tighten the top set screw to hold the blade firmly. The bottom of the blade should float in the air freely, just above the bottom set screw and pad. *(Fig. 2)*

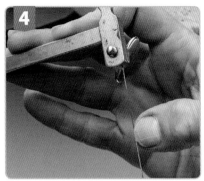

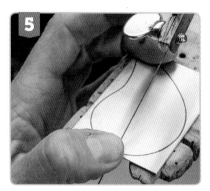

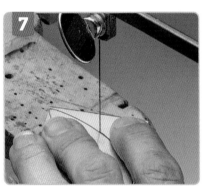

3. Insert the top of the saw frame, with the blade facing up, into the **mandrel hole** of the bench, or position the top bar of the frame against the lip of the bench or work surface. Push slightly against the bottom of the frame handle with your hip, shoulder, or sternum. The bottom bar of the frame will move closer to the bottom of the blade. Push gently until you can capture and insert the blade between the pad and the frame. Tighten the bottom set screw securely, while maintaining pressure on the frame. Release pressure on the frame slowly. *(Fig. 3)*

4. Verify the blade is tight by "pinging" it with your fingernail. It should make a clear, musical sound. If it doesn't, it is too slack and you'll have to adjust the frame to increase tension on the blade. To do this, with the blade still in position, loosen the frame set screw. Hold the frame in your hand with the back of the frame against the heel of your hand. Pull down on the bottom bar with your fingers to increase tension on the blade. Tighten the frame set screw and test the ping of the blade again. It should be high and clear. *(Fig. 4)*

5. To make your first cut, hold the saw in your dominant hand. Position the frame at a 45° angle to the sheet, next to the line, and place your nondominant thumb over the spine of the blade. Gently stroke upward to create a score where you intend to cut. Repeat 2 or 3 times. *(Fig. 5)*

6. Position the saw vertically. Hold the frame loosely, lock the wrist, and begin to move the saw up and down a small amount until the kerf has been started. When you have a good start, begin to saw using the entire length of the blade. Go slow and do not push forward or down, and do not twist the blade. The saw blade should move freely, like a sewing machine needle in steady motion. *(Fig. 6)*

7. Guide the metal by holding it with the index and middle fingers of the nondominant hand on either side of the blade. Steer the metal, not the saw. Slow down when you get to the edge of the sheet and let the cut metal fall away from the blade. When the metal on both sides of the kerf is held too tightly, it gets pinched and won't move freely. The best thing to do in that case is to let go of everything. Then, position the saw and metal on the bench pin and gently pull down on the frame handle. Usually, the blade will free itself, although it may break instead. Either way, it gets unstuck. *(Fig. 7)*

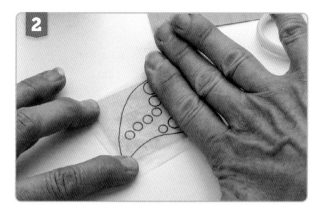

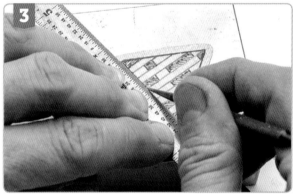

Attaching or scribing a sawing pattern on metal

When sawing, the pattern must be adhered to the sheet or scribed into its surface. It is essential to have a plan before you saw. The more complex a sawing pattern, the more decisions need to be made, including what to cut in which order, which side of a drawn line will be cut, and what areas of metal will be removed when.

There are many ways to transfer a design or pattern, but I find this method the easiest:

1. Photocopy a drawing, trim the excess paper, and coat the back of the paper with a thin coat of rubber cement. Let the cement dry completely. *(Fig. 1)*

2. Brush a thin coat of rubber cement on clean, dry metal and let the cement dry. Then, carefully roll the paper onto the metal, pressing the dried cement sides together so they bond. Start at one edge of the pattern and continue across, taking care not to wrinkle the paper as you roll it onto the metal sheet. *(Fig. 2)*

Another method for transferring a pattern, particularly one composed of straight lines:

3. Draw cutting lines on the metal using a straightedge and a black marker.

4. Re-mark the centers of the drawn marker lines with a scribe. The scribed line will be bright and shiny against the marker line and will not rub off as cutting progresses. *(Fig. 3)*

APPLIED TECHNIQUE:
Sawing the Practice Pattern

It is important to saw often to develop good sawing technique. Progress through this exercise several times using 20-gauge metal sample squares in order of hardness: start with soft aluminum, progress to copper, then jeweler's bronze and finally, cartridge brass. Once you have sawn through the pattern several times with several types of metal and can stay on the lines and not break too many blades, you will have the confidence to progress to precious metal.

Sawing straight lines is a great place to begin. You must decide if you are going to saw on the right edge or the left edge of the line and then do so consistently. As you practice, check your work often.

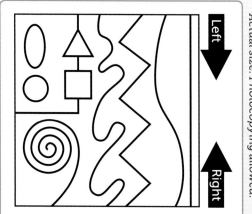

Actual size. Photocopying allowed.

Left

Right

1. Attach the practice pattern to a 2" × 2" (5 × 5 cm) 20-gauge aluminum sheet. Position the metal on the bench pin according to whichever is your dominant hand. *(Fig. 1)*

2. Thread a 2/0 blade into your frame. If you are new to sawing, keep the rest of the blade bundle nearby—you will break at least one blade. Take a deep breath and relax your hands and arms. Exhale. *(Fig. 2)*

3. Cut the entire length of the straight line. *(Fig. 3)*

4. Continue sawing all of the practice lines in order, progressing until you get to the zigzag line. *(Fig. 4)*

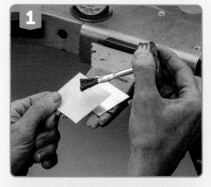

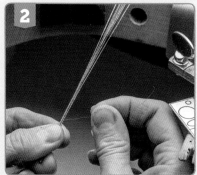

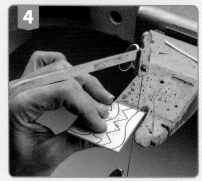

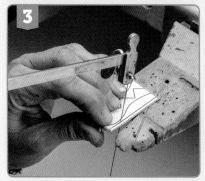

Special techniques for inside and outside corners

After you've sawn the straight, gently curved, and tightly curved lines, you'll need to saw the inside and outside corners of the zigzag line. These are the hardest cuts to master, especially in thicker gauges or harder metals. It is difficult to make the turns and maintain accuracy on a zigzag cut. The most important tip for these sawing scenarios is to pivot the metal in place around the blade at the same time you are moving the saw.

1. Move the saw blade up and down in short strokes and pivot the corner point of the cutting line around the blade until the teeth are facing the direction you want to saw next. Sharp direction changes are very difficult to master, so do not become discouraged. *(Fig. 1)*

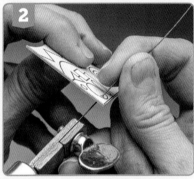

Sawing out the holes

Cutting a hole is easy—once you determine the intended sawing direction. You must drill a pilot hole near the cutting line in a position that allows an efficient transition directly into the cutting outline without a sharp direction change. For complex designs, saw out the innermost openings first, working toward the exterior of the design so the intact exterior metal supports the piece as you work. Because I am right-handed,

I position the opening I am sawing to the left of the blade. If you are left-handed, do the opposite.

1. Make a dot with a marker near the cutting line. Center-punch the dot on steel, then place it on wood and drill using a small, sharp bit that will drill a hole slightly larger than the diameter of the saw blades. *(Fig. 1)*

2. Unscrew the bottom set screw of the frame and string the metal onto the blade with the pattern facing away from you

(toward the top of the frame). Slide it all the way up the blade. *(Fig. 2)*

3. Thread the bottom of the blade as usual. Make sure the blade is under tension. Slide the metal down to the bench pin and start sawing toward the cutting line in a gentle curve. Continue to follow the pattern outline, once you have sawn to it. Remove the completed piece from the saw by releasing the bottom set screw and sliding off the metal. *(Fig. 3)*

Using snips and shears

Snips, shears, and scissors are great time-savers for removing metal quickly—if you treat them with respect. This type of cut produces sharp edges and great force is applied—plus the ensuing sharp bits of flying metal can be harmful. It is essential to protect your hands and eyes with gloves and goggles.

1. Keep your fingers well away from the blades to prevent injury, and never remove the safety spring from the handles of the snips to avoid pinching the heel of the hand during cutting. *(Fig. 1)*

2. To use the snips, insert sheet into the jaws and gently press the handles. *(Fig. 2)*

3. Never snip all the way to the end of the jaws during cutting. Instead, open the jaws and slide the metal in toward the blades for the next cut. The snips should only snap shut on the very last cut. *(Fig. 3 & 4)*

Drilling uniform holes

Taking the time to make a careful layout will pay off in the long run when drilling. To drill a series of uniform holes, it is essential to position the center points accurately. If a large opening is needed, start with a very small drill bit, go all the way through the sheet after center-punching it, and then progress to a larger bit until the target opening size has been drilled. This allows gradual adjustments: a large and badly positioned hole will quickly ruin the work, so work slowly to save time in the long run. For holes larger than about 1/8" (3 mm) in diameter, it is preferable to saw out the opening.

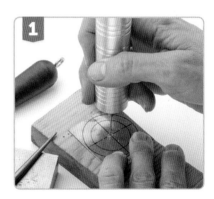

1. Center-punch the center point by marking an X and scribing the final hole size on the sheet. Drill over a scrap of wood to protect the drill bit and the work surface. Progress up through several bit sizes to the final one to avoid dulling the cutting edges. Also, do not allow the drill bit to get hot or it will lose its **temper** and become dull. *(Fig. 1)*

BUILDING BLOCK FOUR:
Filing, Abrading, and Polishing

TOOLS USED IN THIS SECTION:
Sandpaper, abrasive pads, stones, files, needle files, burs, drill bits, pads, compounds

CROSS-REFERENCES:
Material Preparation, *page 31*
Metal Texturing and Surface Embellishment, *page 93*
Brazing and Soldering, *page 79*

For centuries, jewelry was handmade. Traditional hand tools and techniques continue to be widely used today. Thanks to industry and invention, there are also automated ways to perform many of these tasks.

Filing, abrading, and finishing metal are three areas where machine power greatly reduces the amount of time spent on monotonous or time-intensive tasks. However, the trade-off for speed can be loss of control and overly aggressive removal of metal. It is important to practice with power tools on base metals before using them on valuable metals. Practicing with hand tools and techniques before progressing to power tools is wise: learning the order in which to work will eventually become intuitive and will aid you in establishing control of the power tools. There is no substitute for working in the proper order to refine and finish metal to attain the surface you desire.

Jewelry Refinement and Finishing by Hand

PROCESS	DESCRIPTION
SHAPE	Saw/form metal to desired shape
REFINE	Hand file progression; remove defects: cut 1, 2, 3, 4, 5, 6
SMOOTH	Sandpaper progression: 320-grit, 400-grit, 600-grit
FINISH	Polish paper progression: micron 9, 3, 2, 1

Filing

HAND FILES are used to refine fully fabricated work or parts. Both the shape and the surface of the metal can be developed with files, so it is important to have a selection of files with different **profiles**, **sections**, and **cuts** to have the greatest number of options. *The most important rule of thumb for filing is to use the largest tool you can to get the job done.* Then, progress to a smaller tool for refinements. Good filing technique takes time to master, and there are many exercises to help you learn.

Do not file away large amounts of metal when another tool could be used more efficiently, like a saw or scraper.

All files are manufactured to cut on the forward stroke. Excessive force is unnecessary; only use the pressure needed to keep the teeth in contact with the metal and to cut with steady, even strokes. Whenever possible, use the entire length of the file for each stroke to prevent one area of the teeth from wearing out faster than others. On a backward stroke, lift the file because you have to bring the file back to the original position to keep going: dragging the file on the backward stroke dulls its teeth. Position the work on the bench pin from about 6" to 8" (15 to 20.5 cm) away to be able to see well and file efficiently. Progress to finer cuts of file as the work takes form. Essentially, filing is the process of removing large scratches in the metal surface by making smaller scratches over them. Visible scratches eventually become smaller and less visible: only when they do should the next finer size of file be used.

Hand files

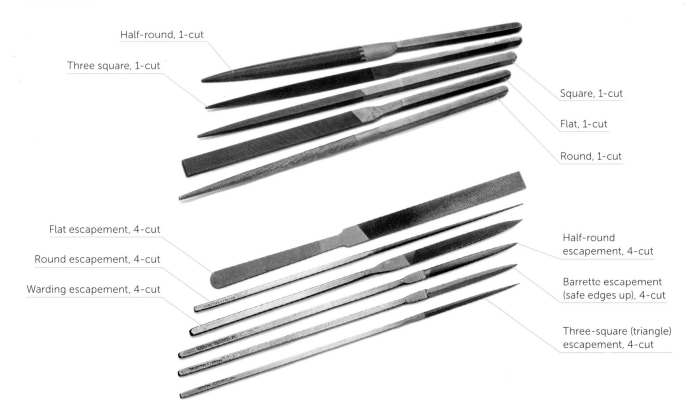

Half-round, 1-cut

Three square, 1-cut

Square, 1-cut

Flat, 1-cut

Round, 1-cut

Flat escapement, 4-cut

Round escapement, 4-cut

Warding escapement, 4-cut

Half-round escapement, 4-cut

Barrette escapement (safe edges up), 4-cut

Three-square (triangle) escapement, 4-cut

There are many families of files for metalwork. For the most part, files of the **Swiss pattern file group** are widely used for jewelry making. This family of files ranges in size from about 8" (20.5 cm) down to the specialty escapement files, where the cutting surface ranges from about ¾" (2 cm) up to about 2" (5 cm) long. All of them are held in the hand. The term **HAND FILES** refers to several groups of tools: **square-tanged**, larger files with a total length of more than 6" (15 cm); **round-tanged** needle files, ranging between 4" (10 cm) to almost 8" (20.5 cm); and specialty files, such as the tiny **escapement** files and **curvilinear riffler** files. Large hand files with square tangs are often inserted into wood or plastic handles for better cushioning during use. Needle and specialty files have round tangs for improved hand comfort.

STEEL ROTARY FILES or **BURS** are attachments used in conjunction with a **FLEXIBLE-SHAFT** machine (usually referred to as a **flex shaft**). These tips perform many of the same tasks that hand files would be used for, except under power. Great care must be taken with these tools, because metal removal is rapid, and the high-speed steel or carbide they are manufactured from will cut softer metals quickly. Always wear eye protection when using these tools.

Hand files (con't.)

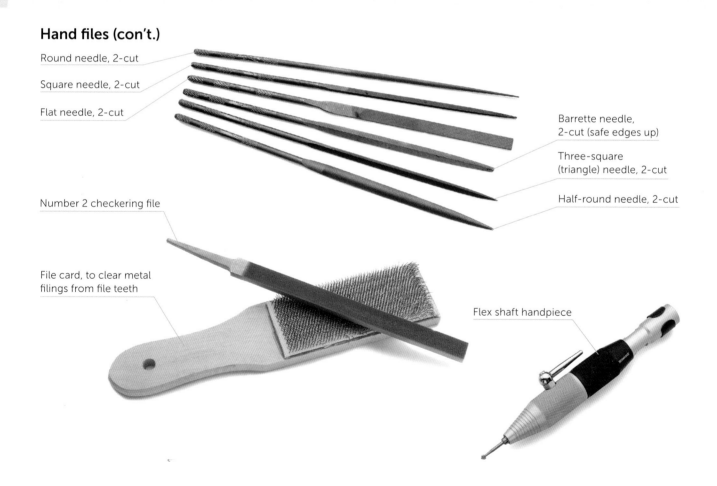

Round needle, 2-cut

Square needle, 2-cut

Flat needle, 2-cut

Barrette needle, 2-cut (safe edges up)

Three-square (triangle) needle, 2-cut

Half-round needle, 2-cut

Number 2 checkering file

File card, to clear metal filings from file teeth

Flex shaft handpiece

Abrading and polishing

ABRASIVES are natural or manufactured grinding mediums used for smoothing metal and to prepare final surfaces. Most often, the **abrasive compound** is bonded to a paper, cloth, or leather backing to be used by hand or machine. Unlike a file, **ABRASIVE PAPERS** will work when used in any direction. Loose **ABRASIVE GRITS** are used in sandblasting or tumble-finishing techniques. Some abrasives are used in stick form in their natural state—Scotch stone and Arkansas stone, for example, or are manufactured into stick form—carborundum and alundum stones. Abrasive stones are used by hand with water to remove scratches and smooth metal surfaces. Abrasive papers—sandpapers—can be used wet or dry, but abrasive compounds suspended in an oil-based or greasy carrier are used only on dry fiber, cloth, or leather.

Rotary files

Abrasive stones

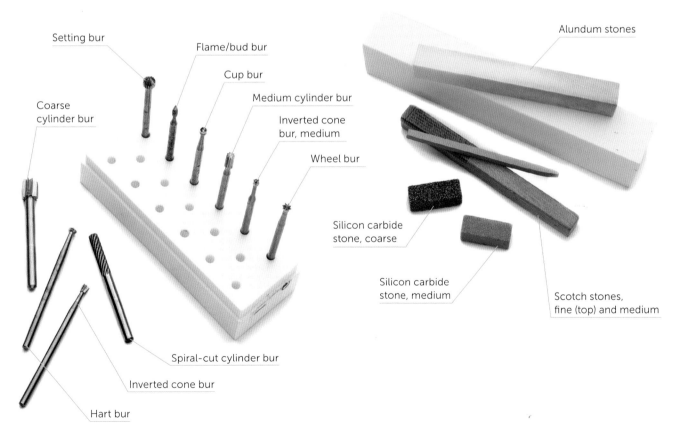

Setting bur

Flame/bud bur

Cup bur

Coarse cylinder bur

Medium cylinder bur

Inverted cone bur, medium

Wheel bur

Spiral-cut cylinder bur

Inverted cone bur

Hart bur

Alundum stones

Silicon carbide stone, coarse

Silicon carbide stone, medium

Scotch stones, fine (top) and medium

ABRASIVE PAPERS include **micro-finishing films** and specialty **polishing cloths**. These are relatively recent products and feature carefully graded compounds and polishing mediums that impregnate a cloth or synthetic paper or fiber carrier. The abrasive grits in these products are graded down to a specific micron measurement, ranging from 100 (the coarsest) to 1. They can be used wet or dry and produce a very fine surface by hand or machine.

These products can also be mounted in the flex shaft and they share many features with other types of abrasive tips. Abrasive papers and polishing cloths and compounds are less aggressive than rotary files and abrasive tips; however, they, too, remove metal faster than by hand. Again, eye protection is required.

Clean Finishing

Many steps are required during the making of jewelry and it is important to continually refine work as it is constructed. During fabrication, it is wise to clean-finish as you go. Each major division of work has an associated typical clean finishing method, so it is important to clean-finish before proceeding to the next division. It is often difficult or even impossible to go back to correct a neglected clean up when making jewelry.

- File and then sand away any defects in the metal stock before cutting it out.

- After sawing or drilling, file and then sand the metal to the pattern lines and remove any deformation or burrs left by the tools.

- After soldering, file and then sand away excess solder and/or solder "ghosts" from the join and/or the surrounding metal.

- Always bring all parts up to at least a 600-grit sanded finish prior to joining them to other parts.

- In general, clean-finished work is clean, smooth, precise, and defect free.

Abrasive papers

Micromesh bonded abrasive films

3M polishing papers

ABRASIVE TIPS are manufactured attachments used with a flex shaft. They feature grits that are mixed with flexible materials such as silicone, plastic, rubber, or fiber, or rigid materials including epoxy or resin. There are also paper-backed grits to mount on specific drum-shaped or wheel-shaped tips. Abrasive tips are used under power and, like rotary files, must be used with great care, because material removal is rapid. Always wear eye protection during their use.

Other machine-driven abrasive methods include grinding wheels and belt sanders. They are seldom used on precious metal, but can be very effective on steel and harder metals. Often, these power tools are used with steel rod to make punches, stamps, and other tools, or to modify manufactured hand tools for custom applications.

Abrasive tips

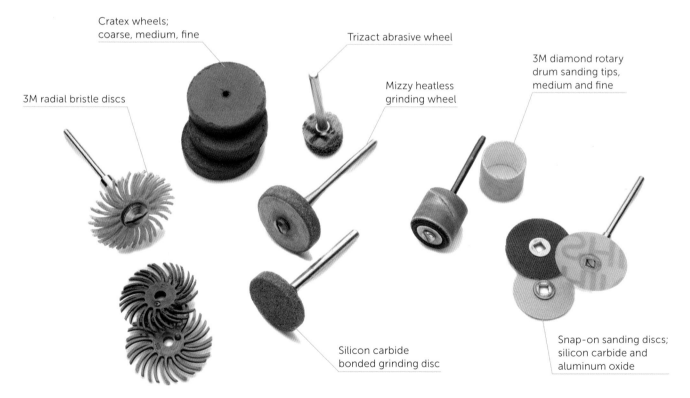

Cratex wheels; coarse, medium, fine

Trizact abrasive wheel

3M diamond rotary drum sanding tips, medium and fine

Mizzy heatless grinding wheel

3M radial bristle discs

Silicon carbide bonded grinding disc

Snap-on sanding discs; silicon carbide and aluminum oxide

Common File Profiles and Sections

Dotted lines are cutting surfaces; solid lines are safe edges.

COMMON FILE PROFILES

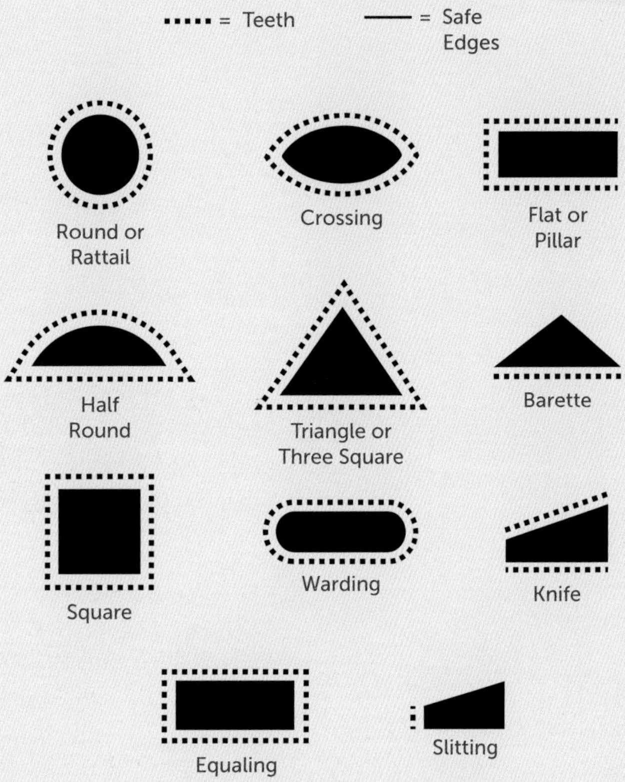

····· = Teeth   **——— = Safe Edges**

Round or Rattail

Crossing

Flat or Pillar

Half Round

Triangle or Three Square

Barette

Square

Warding

Knife

Equaling

Slitting

PARTS OF A FILE

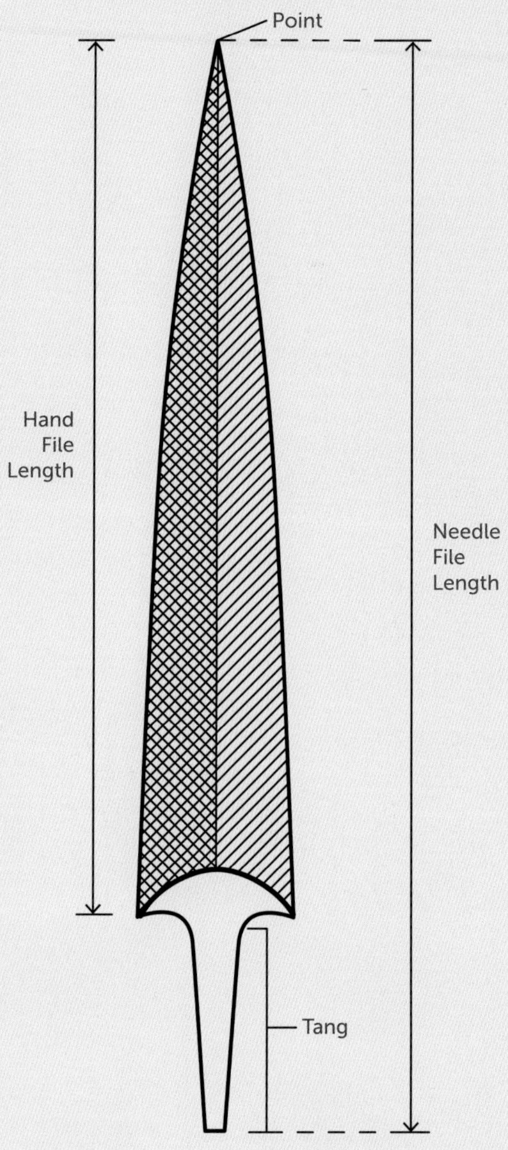

Point

Hand File Length

Needle File Length

Tang

When to File

- Remove burrs from sawn or pierced edges and openings
- Trim a sawn line to true position or dimension
- Enlarge drilled openings
- Shape corners, slits, or slots
- Remove errant solder
- Bevel edges
- Create decorative cuts or surfaces
- Refine solder seams and joins

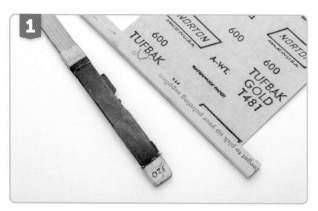

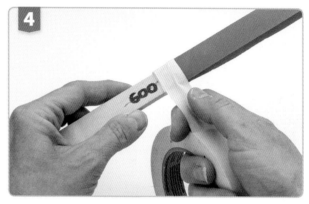

How to make a sanding stick

Take the time to make several sanding sticks of different grits for quick touch-ups as you work. A good sanding stick will last several years if you carefully scribe the fold lines to allow for easy tear-off as the paper is worn through use.

1. Lay a half-sheet of abrasive paper on a flat surface, grit-side down. Position a flat strip of wood, such as a paint stirrer, along the closest edge of the paper. *(Fig. 1)*

2. Gently run a scribe along the other edge of the wood strip to score, but not cut, the abrasive paper. *(Fig. 2)*

3. Grip the paper firmly and roll the strip of wood toward the scored line to create a fold.

Keep repeating the score/ fold/roll process until the entire sheet of paper has been rolled onto the strip of wood. *(Fig. 3)*

4. Tape the ends of the paper to the stick with masking tape. Label the grit on the stick with a marker. As needed, remove a layer by tearing off the worn paper along the scored fold line cleanly and discarding it. *(Fig. 4)*

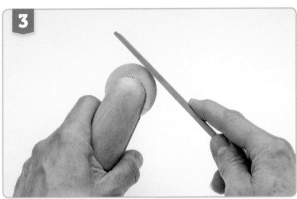

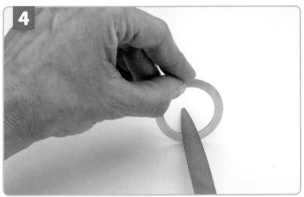

How to file

Differently shaped edges call for different file profiles. No matter what you are filing, it is important to support the work as steadily as possible. Do not "air file"—doing so will create uneven surfaces in the metal. Use a vise, clamp, or your bench pin to hold the work steady as you file.

Filing straight, flat edges

1. The file must be guided perfectly straight. Choose the longest file you have and progress to smaller, shorter files only when restricted by the size of the work. Without applying excessive pressure, place your index finger on top of the file and push forward over as long a distance as possible to avoid creating unwanted depressions in the surface. *(Fig. 1)*

2. Change the direction of the filing by rotating the work often; a close look at the reflective area created by the file will reveal areas that need more work. For very large flat edges, clamp the metal in a vise and guide a large flat file with both hands to prevent curving strokes and rounded corners. *(Fig. 2)*

Filing curved surfaces

1. A file must move along an arc, away from the body. If the piece is small, hold it in a hand vise, ring clamp, or pin vise. Again, for even filing, choose the largest size file you can use for the work required. To steady the work, brace the hand holding the work against the bench pin as you file across the curve. *(Fig. 3)*

2. For filing concave curves, use round, half-round, or riffler files in a size appropriate to the curve. For convex curves, a flat file is usually sufficient. *(Fig. 4)*

How to use a rotary file

Take care when using power to remove metal. The flex shaft can be a great time-saver: however, supporting the work well is essential, as well as slow, steady use of the bur to avoid damage to the metal. Goggles are a safety essential when using the flex shaft.

1. Carefully insert the bur into the hand piece and use the **chuck key** to tighten it. With the hand piece on the bench top, verify that the attachment is inserted correctly by lightly stepping on the power pedal. The tip should not wiggle, wobble, or come loose. A properly inserted tip will spin evenly and remain centered and parallel to the work surface. *(Fig. 1)*

2. Position the work and the hand piece for maximum support. Try to have the work, the hand piece, and most of the hand holding the hand piece supported on the bench top. *(Fig. 2)*

3. Work very slowly to avoid damage to the tool and the work. Use a bur lubricant to avoid overheating the cutting edges of the attachment—which will damage the temper of the tool steel, resulting in a dull cutting edge and a shorter life. Allow the tool to cool by lifting it often and clearing debris from the opening. *(Fig. 3)*

APPLIED TECHNIQUE:
Change the Profile of Stock by Filing

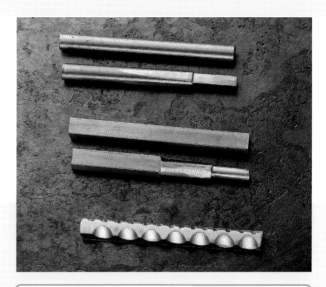

Changing the profile of stock metal is a great way to practice filing. Work carefully and strive for precision when changing the shape of the metal rod.

Three exercises to develop filing technique:

1. **Square stock to round:** Start with a 2" (5 cm) length of 5 mm square brass stock. Scribe 2 points on the stock—at ½" (1.3 cm) in from one edge, and at 1" (2.5 cm). Beginning at the 1" (2.5 cm) mark, use a flat file to "knock off" the corners of the stock to create an even-sided octagonal profile all the way across the remaining stock. At the ½" (1.3 cm) mark, knock off the corners of the octagon to create an even circle on one-half of the originally square stock.

2. **Round stock to square:** Start with a 2" (5 cm) length of 6 mm round brass rod. As above, scribe a line at ½" (1.3 cm) and at 1" (2.5 cm). Starting at the 1" (2.5 cm) mark, use a flat file to create 4 evenly spaced tapered "facets" all the way across the remainder of the rod. At the ½" (1.3 cm) mark, reduce the profile further to create a well-defined and centered square.

3. **Facets and cuts in square stock:** Start with a 2" (5 cm) length of 5 mm square brass stock. Scribe a line every ¼" (6 mm). On the corner, between faces 4 and 1, use the curved face of a half-round file to create evenly placed, scalloped facets of the same depth centered on each scribe mark. On the corner between faces 2 and 3, use a three-square file to create evenly spaced, sharp-edged facets of the same depth centered on each scribe mark. For advanced practice, "knock off" the entire sharp corner of the edge of faces 1 and 2 to a 45° angle. Do this also for the corner between faces 3 and 4, and then, with a round needle file, create evenly spaced small hemispherical indents along the entire edge.

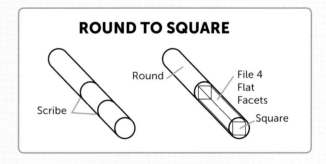

SQUARE TO ROUND

ROUND TO SQUARE

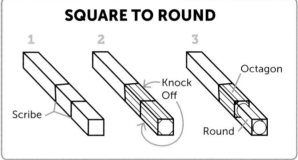

FACETS AND CUTS

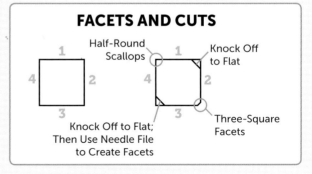

Common Rotary Files and Burs

Every bur shape is manufactured in a range of sizes and materials, including both carbon and carbide steel, tungsten, and vanadium steel. There are several shank sizes available, with ⅛" (3 mm) or ³⁄₃₂" (2.5 mm) being the most common. Generally, larger tips have larger shanks to avoid breakage, and most are available for quick-change hand pieces.

Shape	Description	Purpose
1. CUP	Indented with interior cutting edge	Prong finishing; bead and granule refinement
2. WHEEL	Short, disc-like version of cylinder	Gemstone settings; cleanup; metal removal
3. BUD OR FLAME	Spindle-shaped; also called flame	Slight curved grooves or openings with angled bottoms; carving
4. BALL	Can be round, pear, or oval in profile	Round-bottomed openings or grooves, dish- or bowl-shaped openings
5. INVERTED CONE	Wide at tip; tapering toward shank	Undercutting channels or grooves for inlay, cleanup
6. CYLINDER	Nontapered cylinder	Rapid metal removal; cleanup
7. SETTING	Cone-shaped point or cylindrical base	Creating settings for faceted round gemstones
8. CONE	Straight-sided	Severely tapered grooves or openings; for enlarging drilled openings
9. KNIFE	Sharply tapered disc	Undercutting; cleanup; creating channels

1   2   3   4   5   6   7   8   9

PART FOUR:
Fabrication and Assembly

BUILDING BLOCK FIVE:
Cold Connections

TOOLS USED IN THIS SECTION:
Riveting hammer, riveting punches, rivet block, tap and die, ball daps, drills, flex shaft, drill gauge, wire gauge, tube-cutting jig, files, abrasives

CROSS-REFERENCES:
Material Preparation, *page 31*
Holding Your Work, *page 37*
Brazing and Soldering, *page 79*
Drilling Uniform Holes, *page 55*
Links and Units, *page 130*

Cold connections are among the most exciting and innovative ways to join various materials without the use of a torch and without glue or adhesives.

Connectors such as rivets, tabs, stitches, folds, and wraps are versatile and visually intriguing methods for connecting jewelry elements and are the best method for connecting delicate or flammable materials.

It can be just as or even more challenging to join a well-planned and skillfully executed piece without fire as for a soldered one. You'll find it invaluable to master the construction of rivets and many other kinds of cold joins before advancing to soldering, because solving the mental challenges of fabricating fragile materials using a difficult sequence of techniques can ultimately be very rewarding.

Cold connection tools

The essentials for riveting and other cold connections include twist drills, gauges, a variety of punches and blocks, as well as the riveting hammer.

Rivets

Every type of **RIVET** has the same function: they are all metal plugs that are manipulated with tools to fill a hole or holes in other objects to hold them together. Rivets have many shapes but are one of two types: solid or hollow. Both types of rivets can be either fixed **(press-fit)** or movable **(running-fit)**. Rivet heads can be raised above the surrounding surface and be plain or decorative. When rivets are flush with the metal surface, they are called **blind rivets**.

With the exception of blind rivets, all parts to be connected must be fabricated and finished before the rivets are set and finally secured. Keep in mind when constructing your piece that blind rivets are filed and sanded at the same time as the surrounding surface.

PRESS-FIT RIVETS are immobile. They are set and firmly secured once the piece has been completely fabricated to prevent any movement in the parts.

Cold connection tools

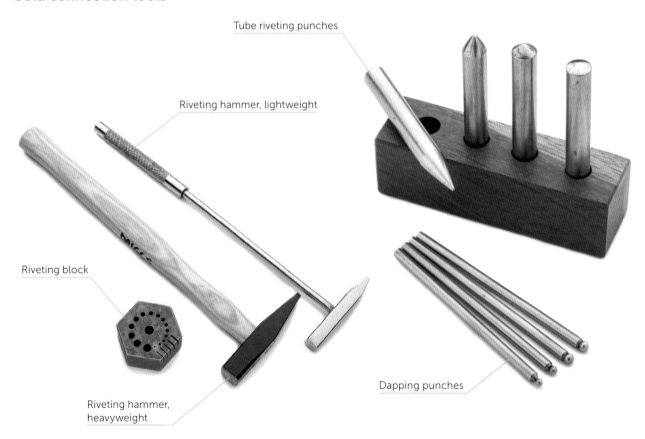

Tube riveting punches

Riveting hammer, lightweight

Riveting block

Riveting hammer, heavyweight

Dapping punches

RUNNING-FIT RIVETS permit sections of metal to pivot or move around their shanks. They are created by inserting a strip of paper or card stock between the layers of the work before setting and securing the tail of the rivet. Once the tail of the rivet is **planished** (smoothed by hammering lightly), the paper spacer is removed, leaving a small space that allows movement.

Common Steps for Every Rivet

No matter what shape, size, or type they are, rivets are always installed following these steps:

1. Prepare all layers of the parts to be connected.

2. Measure the rivet diameter.

3. Create holes in the parts to be attached that match the rivet diameter.

4. Flare or create a head on one end of the rivet using a riveting hammer.

5. Test-fit the rivet and cut any excess length.

6. Set the rivet.

7. Repeat Steps 1–6 to set remaining rivets.

8. Secure all rivets by hammering evenly around the piece.

Cold connection tools (con't.)

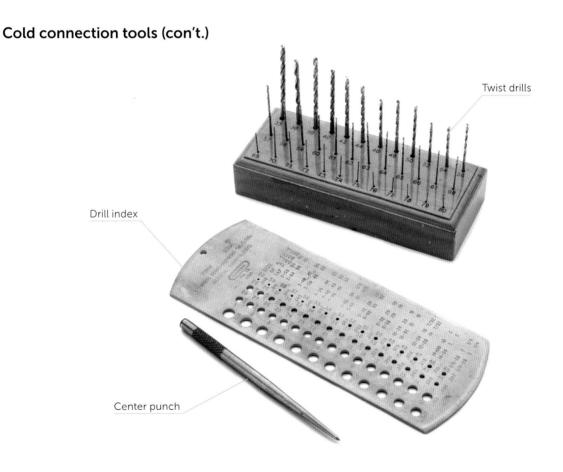

Twist drills

Drill index

Center punch

Types and Styles of Rivets

SOLID RIVET PARTS: head, shank, tail

RIVET HEAD SHAPES: button, flat, cone, square

BLIND RIVETS are flush with metal surface. Also called countersunk rivets

TUBE RIVET PARTS: top flange, shaft, bottom flange

FLANGES can be plain, divided, or shaped.

SLIDING or **ALMAIN RIVETS** fit within a groove or slot and can be fixed or removable.

SPLIT RIVETS, also called studs, brads, or integral rivets, have a U-shaped shaft and large head.

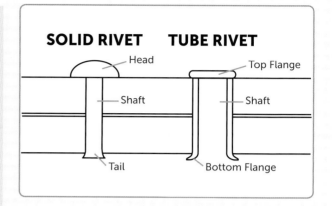

SOLID RIVET   TUBE RIVET

Head · Top Flange · Shaft · Shaft · Tail · Bottom Flange

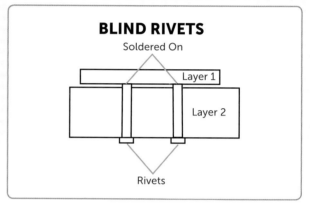

BLIND RIVETS

Soldered On · Layer 1 · Layer 2 · Rivets

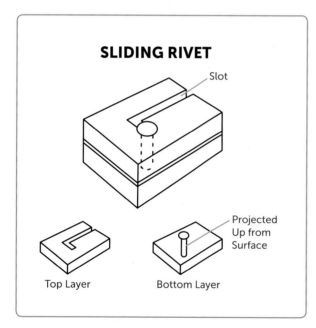

SLIDING RIVET

Slot · Projected Up from Surface · Top Layer · Bottom Layer

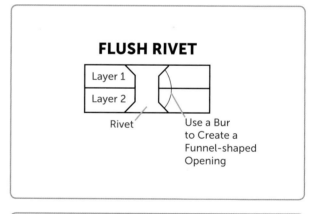

FLUSH RIVET

Layer 1 · Layer 2 · Rivet · Use a Bur to Create a Funnel-shaped Opening

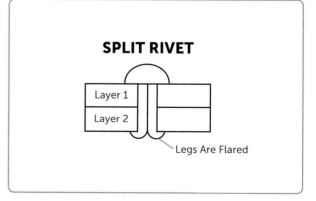

SPLIT RIVET

Layer 1 · Layer 2 · Legs Are Flared

Other cold connections

TABS are tongues of metal, raised or lowered from the body of the piece, which hold elements together by pressure or tension. Tabs may be decorative or plain and can take many shapes.

FOLDS hold metal elements together by tension. Metal malleability and geometry can be used to design clever connections based on folds.

SCREWS and **BOLTS** can be created with a tap and die to fabricate screw threads on the surface of a rod. Threads can be cut on the inside of a drilled hole to create a "bolt" of any shape or size.

WRAPS and **STITCHES** are methods of holding metal together based on fiber arts techniques. Lashing, knotting, netting, splicing, and coiling can all be used with wire and metal sheet.

JUMP RINGS are links that connect adjacent units through openings. They can be many shapes and sizes, but all jump rings begin as an open unit of wire or sheet with a sawn kerf. After joining, jump rings may be soldered, fused (fine silver only), or left unsoldered.

Cold connections are a versatile method for joining delicate or flammable materials. They include stitches, hardware, middle folds, tube rivets, and tabs.

Stitches

Hardware

Tube rivet plus fold

Folds

Folds

Tabs

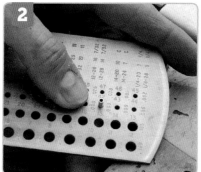

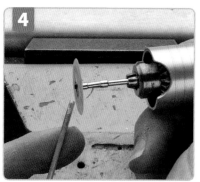

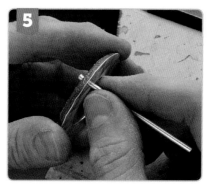

How to make and set a tube rivet

Manufactured thin-walled seamless tubing makes fabricating clean tube rivets easy. A set of gently pointed or cone-shaped punches will make forming the rivet easier, but a center punch or dapping punches in small sizes will work just as well.

Tube rivets are the easiest rivets to fabricate. Traditionally, these rivets are created with seamless tubing. Purchase thin-walled seamless tubing—thick-walled tubing will work but is more challenging. The most difficult part of fabricating well-made tube rivets is to cut the tubing to the correct length and finish cleanly for a smooth roll on both sides of the rivet.

1. Prepare the layers you intend to rivet. File, sand, and pre-polish all the various parts. Mark the positions for the rivets, but do not drill them yet. *(Fig. 1)*

2. For a secure rivet, the tubing you choose must just pass through the drilled holes. Measure the outer diameter of the tubing. A handy tool for this task is a **drill index** or **digital calipers**. Center-punch and drill only the first rivet hole of the top layer. If you don't have a drill bit of the same diameter as the tubing (which often will be the situation) you must use a saw, bur, or round file to enlarge the opening to the correct diameter. File and sand burrs away from both sides of the sheet. *(Fig. 2)*

3. Stack the drilled top layer over the bottom layer and mark the hole position on the latter. Drill the lower layer, refine the opening, and remove burrs. Check the fit of the tubing through both layers—it should be snug, but not too tight. *(Fig. 3)*

4. Sand or file one end of the tubing to ensure it is cut cleanly, is perpendicular, and is burr-free. Do not skip this finishing step: a well-finished rivet is worth the extra effort. Without cutting the other end of the tubing, flare the prepared end with a center punch, awl, or pointed riveting punch. The easiest way to do this is to hold the tool at a slight angle and go around in a circle one direction several times, then back the other way. *(Fig. 4)*

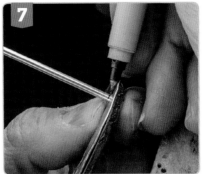

5. Insert the unflared end of the tubing through both layers of the piece from the top to confirm that the flared end will not pass through the hole. If it does pass through, you must expand its collar by flaring it more until it does not pass through. Work slowly and deliberately to keep an even flare and a circular shape. *(Fig. 5)*

6. When the flare is satisfactory, hold the layers together firmly and push the flared end of the tubing tightly against the top of the piece. *(Fig. 6)*

7. Working from the back of the piece, mark a cutting line on the tubing. Typically, the thickness of a fine-line marker nib is about the right measure at which to cut the tubing.

Remove the tubing and cut in a perpendicular line with a fine saw blade. File and sand the cut end, taking care to keep the cut perpendicular to the tube and to remove all burrs. *(Fig. 7)*

8. Reinsert the rivet and hold the layers together with masking tape as you set the back of the rivet. *(Fig. 8)*

9. Flare the back of the rivet the same way you did for the front. Continue flaring until the rivet is secure. The rivet is set when it won't fall out.

At this point, drill and set all remaining rivets on the piece. After you have set the first rivet, you may drill through all layers at once: ensure the positions of the layers are correct before you do. If there are many rivets, work back and forth across the piece to keep the tension evenly distributed. *(Fig. 9)*

10. Once all rivets have been set, you are ready to secure them. Use a small **ball dap** or **conical riveting punch** to compress the tubing tightly against the piece. Work a few taps on the front, then flip the piece over and work a few taps on the back. Continue by moving to each successive rivet across the piece and compress in the same way. The goal is to compress all of the rivets equally so the top layer is pushed against the bottom layer evenly. **Planish** the tops of the finished rivets gently with a highly polished planishing or riveting hammer to remove any lingering tool marks. *(Fig. 10)*

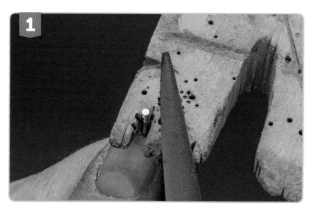

How to make and set a solid rivet

Solid rivets are more difficult to create than tube rivets, because you must hammer well while holding the wire at just the right place to create the rivet heads. Use 12- to 16-gauge wire, but no smaller (it is likely thinner wire will bend). Follow the directions for making the rivet holes and positioning the layers in Steps 1–3 on page 74. Next, follow these steps to fabricate nicely shaped wire rivets and rivet heads.

1. Drill a hole that matches the wire diameter, as described previously. Heat the wire to anneal, then cut a 1" (2.5 cm) to 2" (5 cm) length. It is critical to file the cut end so it is exactly 90° to the shaft of the rivet (i.e., perpendicular), smooth, round, and burr-free. Round rivet heads should be *round*. Misshapen wire edges will worsen when you hammer them flatter and larger. *(Fig. 1)*

2. Hold the wire in toothed pliers. Using a fine cross-peen, riveting, or goldsmith's hammer, create a series of parallel furrows in the wire end until it begins to spread into an oval. Alternatively, insert the wire into a **rivet block** to form the head. *(Fig. 2)*

3. Rotate the pliers 90°. Hammer a second series of parallel furrows on the same wire end to spread it into a circle with a crosshatched surface. *(Fig. 3)*

4. Test-fit the rivet in the piece. It should not pass through the drilled hole. If it does, you must continue to hammer the end of the wire until the rivet does not pass through the hole. If the wire is very thick or you've had to hammer a lot to create the rivet head, anneal again, pickle, rinse, and dry. *(Fig. 4)*

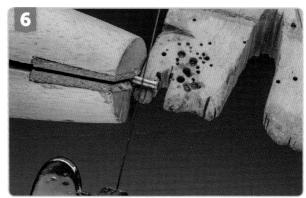

5. Once the rivet head fits, insert the rivet from the front through all layers to be connected and mark a cutting line on the wire at the back of the piece. Again, the thickness of a fine-line marker nib is usually a good margin of metal to leave for the rivet head. If the wire is very thick, leave a bit more metal by cutting just outside of the marked line. *A good rule of thumb is to allow about half the thickness of whatever rivet stock you are using to form a rivet head.* **(Fig. 5)**

6. Remove the rivet wire and saw at the line. Don't be tempted to use nippers or cutters: saw it! A clean rivet head should start as a circle, not a V (which nippers will produce). If you must use nippers, allow a little extra wire and file off the beveled cut until the end of the wire is a clean, flat, round circle. **(Fig. 6)**

7. Insert the cut rivet and secure the layers as in the tube-riveting steps on pages 74–75. Hammer the rivet as before to create a crosshatched round head. Once both sides of the wire have been spread evenly and will not pass through the hole, the wire rivet is set. **(Fig. 7)**

Make and set all remaining rivets in the piece. To finish and secure the wire rivets, turn the riveting hammer to the **planishing face** and smooth the crosshatched surface until it is round and flat. Hammering from top to bottom and from side to side, compress the rivets and the layers of the piece evenly.

APPLIED TECHNIQUE:
A Movable Chain of Units Joined with Rivets

Running-fit rivets allow flat metal units to be combined into an interesting flexible chain. Combinations of metal texture, metal finish, and metal color offer endless variations.

Parts List
- 4 Unit A
- 6 Unit B
- 12 spacers
- 12 rivets

Tools
Saw, circle or disc cutter, center punch, #51 drill bit, flex shaft, riveting hammer, files, sanding sticks, steel block, pliers, millimeter gauge, B & S gauge

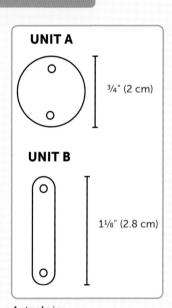

UNIT A

¾" (2 cm)

UNIT B

1⅛" (2.8 cm)

Actual size.

CONSTRUCTION DIAGRAM

Rivet
Top Bar
Insert Paper Here
Spacer 1
Drill
Disc
Spacer 2
Insert Paper Here
Bottom Bar

Saw off excess rod at mark. Create rivet head first.

1. Start with 24-gauge brass or copper sheet.

2. Saw out or use a disc cutter to create 4 Unit A circles (¾" [2 cm] diameter).

3. Saw out 6 Unit B rounded bars (1⅛" [2.5 cm]).

4. Cut twelve 3 mm long sections of ³⁄₃₂" brass or aluminum thin-walled tubing for spacers.

5. With a saw, cut twelve 25 mm long sections of either ¹⁄₁₆"

(2 mm) brass rod or 14-gauge brass or copper wire.

6. File, sand, and clean-finish all cut edges of all parts.

7. With a #51 drill bit, drill holes in all A and B Units where indicated.

8. Create rivet heads on one end of each rod section.

9. Starting with the first Unit A, assemble the units one at a time as shown in the Construction

Diagram. Before setting the rivet tails, insert a strip of index card between the tube spacer and the Unit B bar as shown.

10. Only set the rivets once the entire chain has been fabricated and the rivets are secured. Then, remove the paper with needle-nose pliers and test the movement of the chain. It should move freely and be flexible, with a wavelike motion.

BUILDING BLOCK SIX:
Brazing and Soldering

TOOLS USED IN THIS SECTION:
Torch system, solder station, solder, fluxes, annealing pan, pickle pot, firebricks, tweezers, tongs, third hand, tripod, ring stand, Solderite block, honeycomb block, turntables, charcoal block, various solder forms, brass brush

CROSS-REFERENCES:
Material Preparation, *page 31*
Holding Your Work, *page 37*
Filing, Abrading, and Polishing, *page 56*

Joining nonferrous metal using a torch and a metal filler called **solder** at temperatures above 840°F (449°C) is called **brazing** or **hard-soldering**.

Unlike welding, the metal to be joined is not melted during brazing—only the introduced, nonferrous metal alloy, called solder, melts. In a well-prepared seam or **join**, molten solder flows freely between the parts to create a permanent alloy filler that, when solidified, is almost invisible. This filler is called a **solder fillet**. The fillet connects well into the "grain" of the metal of the join, but no fusion of the materials takes place. In welding, both the filler and the metal adjacent to the join are melted and they coalesce to become one material.

Many variables come into play during soldering. The largest and probably the most important skill set in jewelry making is to master the use of solder grades for different metals in many connection styles and forms. Knowing what part to solder when and with what type of solder takes years of trial and error and experience, so regular practice is essential. A jewelry maker must know the metal, the torch, and the solder well enough to predict the outcome based on past experience. When soldering, there are three stages: **(1)** preparation/cleaning, **(2)** heating/soldering, and **(3)** quenching/pickling. You will achieve successful soldering if you approach each solder join in this order.

HOW TO ANNEAL

Annealing is the term used for reducing the stress in work hardened metal. Heating the metal with a torch or in a kiln to a specific temperature will cause the crystal arrangement within the metal to expand and relax, returning the metal to a more malleable state. Each type of metal has specific annealing guidelines, and experienced metalsmiths can observe the color of the metal as it is heated to know when to quench. Other methods that can be used to determine annealing temperature, such as a black permanent marker dot on the metal prior to heating it, which will burn off at the point the metal is annealed. Or, the metal can be painted with a coat of paste flux; this will turn clear and glassy at about 1100°F which is the proper annealing temperature. When annealing with a torch, it is best to do so in a darkened area to most closely observe the color of the hot metal.

Annealing Guidelines

Process	Metals
Heat metal to a dull red color, then quench in clean, clear water as soon as the redness leaves the metal.	Gold: 14K, 10K, all rose gold; Sterling; Fine silver and Copper.
Heat metal to a dull red color, Do not quench. Allow the metal to air cool.	Argentium sterling.
Heat metal to medium red, then quench in clean, clear water as soon as the redness leaves the metal.	Jeweler's bronze.
Heat to glowing, bright red, but do not quench. Allow the metal to air cool.	Brass, White gold, Nickel.

HOW TO PATINATE

Patina is a general term used for color on metal. Patinas will occur naturally over time on all metals except gold and platinum. With exposure to the elements, natural coloration will occur—or patinas can be induced on metals through the judicious application of heat or chemicals. Generally, texture and patina go hand in hand. The more textured a metal surface, the more successful a patina application will be. The process for successful patination is like many other metalworking processes—each method differs, but most follow these basic steps:

Preparation

- The metal must be clean, free of dust, dirt, oils, compounds, grease, wax, or grime of any kind. Ideally, metal to be patinated will be pickled and freshly washed with soap and water and then rinsed well; after that, handle the metal only by the edges.

- The metal must be dry. Water or other moisture will prevent good contact with the patination agent or chemicals or dilute it.

- The patination solution must be fresh and uncontaminated. Mix it according to manufacturer's specifications just before use.

- The patination work area must be clean and dust free and have adequate ventilation. Dedicated application tools specific to each type of patina should be used and stored in well-labeled containers to keep them clean and to avoid cross-contamination.

Application methods

- Spray on the patina using a pump bottle.

- Brush on the patina with a paintbrush.

- Immerse the entire piece in a bath of patina solution.

- Bury or encase the object in a patina-saturated absorbent material such as sawdust, shredded paper, or cloth.

- Vapor-induce or fume color on the metal by suspending the work above or near the patina chemical in an airtight container.

Finishing methods

- Remove the object from the patina and rinse well in cool running water.

- Gently dry the object well and inspect the patina for evenness.

- Once the desired effect is achieved, seal the metal surface with lacquer or wax to preserve the desired color.

Soldering tools: station tools

Pumice-filled
annealing pan

Charcoal block

Firebrick

Honeycomb
soldering brick

Soldering turntable

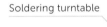

Ring soldering support

Striker

Steel soldering screen

Locking tweezers

Soldering pick

Straight tweezers, fine

Straight tweezers,
extra-fine

SOLDERING TOOLS

Soldering tools can be divided into two categories: station tools and soldering supplies. Every studio must have a torch, pickle pot, and fireproof work area. Other station tools include supports, tweezers, and blocks.

Soldering supplies include paste flux and liquid flux, anti flux (yellow ochre), application tools such as brushes and bottles, and a variety of containers in which to store them.

Types and Forms of Solders

Solder moves by virtue of a scientific condition called **capillarity**, in which a solid surface attracts the molecules of a liquid it is in contact with toward it (it is a natural tendency of liquids to be attracted to solid objects). Once solder becomes molten, its surface tension relaxes, allowing it to flow into the tiniest of openings, always moving toward the heat. A clean and well-fluxed surface creates a smooth pathway that will carry a minute chip of molten solder for a great distance.

Every precious metal alloy has an appropriate **solder alloy** to use with it. For precious metals, it is preferable to use **hard solder**—which melts at high heat and for metals with melting points at higher than 800°F, rather than **soft solder**, which is appropriate for metals with melting points lower than 800°F. The greater strength of hard solder and the very visible color difference in a join made of soft solder make the hard solder a better choice in most jewelry applications. Solder is **graded** according to the temperature range in which it melts. Depending on the alloy it must join, solder is available in several forms: as sheet, wire or rod, paste, and powder. For gold, **plumb solders** are alloyed to match the quality of the gold in karats, as well as the base color.

It is critical to store solders in clearly labeled, airtight containers to avoid tarnish and oxidation. Do not cut more than is needed just before use. Note the grade, type, and manufacturer of the solder on labels, as slight variations in alloying can occur from brand to brand. Before cutting pallions, sand the surface of both sheet and wire solders gently to remove any surface oxidation that would inhibit solder flow.

Soldering supplies

Liquid flux in spray bottle

Paste flux

Liquid flux dispenser

Yellow ochre powder mix, anti-flux

How to solder

Stage 1: Preparing and cleaning a solder join or presoldering

In every solder join, no matter what metal or solder is used, it is absolutely essential to clean the parts and position them correctly so the join will be tight and well made. Once you have mastered the three-stage process, soldering will become a predictable, repeatable, and rewarding experience instead of a lucky accident. Although every soldering operation is unique, here are general guidelines to follow to ensure success.

ALL PARTS MUST FIT TOGETHER WELL. This is easier said than done. Flat surfaces should be flat with no gaps: light should not pass through any opening between the parts. Curved surfaces should also fit with no gaps, and parts must be filed so their curve contours match. In this process, which is called **fitting a join**, the edges must be filed, sanded, and manipulated to join perfectly along every area of every metal part in the join. Ideally, well-prepared parts should sit or balance on their own, without the aid of props, binding wire, or weights, and with only the perfection of their preparation holding them together during the test fit and setup—before the torch is used. The goal is to create as much contact between the parts as possible: the solder should flow quickly along the join due to capillary attraction.

Openings, depressions, gaps, or dips will cause the molten solder to pool and stall at that point of the join. Do not rely on solder to fill a poorly prepared join.

ALL PARTS MUST BE CLEAN. No oxidation, tarnish, dirt, oil, grease, polishing compound, dust, or fingerprints can be present at the join. Pickle, rinse, and dry all metal just before soldering and do not touch the join again with your fingers until it has been soldered.

ALL PARTS MUST BE FLUXED to protect the join from forming oxides during soldering. Flux is a commercially prepared chemical solution or paste that creates a clean and controlled environment to allow molten solder to flow rapidly along an uninterrupted path at the join. Apply only clean and well-mixed flux appropriate to the firing temperature and type of solder and metal. Brush on paste flux with a soft paintbrush dedicated only to that type of flux, or spray liquid fluxes over the parts in a light mist as directed by the manufacturer.

ALL SOLDER MUST BE NEWLY CLEANED AND POSITIONED to anticipate how it will flow once the torch is applied. Use the minimum amount of solder needed to fill a join. Determining the proper amount to use becomes easier with experience: beginners often flood a piece with too much solder. Ideally, snippets—or **pallions**—of solder should be cut as small as is manageable, only when needed, and they should never be thicker than

Types of Torch Flames

Name	Description	Purpose	
REDUCING 🙂 Anneal	Yellowish; bushy and wiggly	Surplus fuel; good for annealing	Reducing—fuel rich; Deep blue cone with orange flecks
NEUTRAL 🙂 Solder Perfect	Balanced fuel and oxygen; pointed, slightly yellow-blue.	In general, the most used flame type for soldering	Neutral—equal; medium blue orange tip
OXIDIZING ☹	Surplus-free oxygen; thin inner cone, clear blue; "hissy"	*Not recommended, except for platinum. Causes excessive **firescale**.*	Oxidizing—fuel starved; purple blue

the parts to be joined. Small solder snippets melt and flow rapidly, so taking the prep time to cut them small will make soldering the join a smoother process.

ALL SOLDERING OPERATIONS SHOULD EXPLOIT GRAVITY WHENEVER POSSIBLE. Solder will follow the torch flame and flow toward the hottest part of the join. On a clean join, this will occur rapidly, even against gravity. For extra ease, position parts to be joined to encourage the molten solder to flow where you want it to with the aid of gravity. Liquid tends to flow downward first, so position joins accordingly. Use binding wire, props, clips, and pins minimally as they will draw heat into them. They are used to prevent warping and movement but should not be relied on as a fix for a poor fit. The heat of the surrounding metal is what causes the solder to melt, so more heat will be required to bring bound parts up to soldering temperature. Position all parts with this in mind.

Stage 2: Heating and soldering a join

Once the metal parts to be soldered have been cleaned, fluxed, and positioned with the desired grade of solder cut, the torch can be lit. There are many types of torches available for jewelry making, ranging from small hand-held micro torches that, largely, burn butane fuel, up to sophisticated fuel and oxygen systems that burn a fuel gas and compressed oxygen supplied from either portable tanks or, in the case of natural gas, a hard-lined system

Types of Common Solder Joins

Joins	Description	Examples	
BUTT JOINS	Two edges squarely come together.	Flat to flat, Flat to curve, Curve to curve	**BUTT JOINS** Butt Joins— Two Edges Come Together, Like to Like Profiles
LAP JOINS	One part overlaps another part or edge.	Flat to flat, Flat to curve, Curve to curve, Sleeve	**LAP JOINS** One Part Overlaps Another Part
NOTCHED JOINS	Parts interlock at join by way of a cut channel, which increases surface contact.	Scarf, Beveled, Slotted	**NOTCHED JOINS** One Part Slides into Another Part and is Soldered
POINT-OF-CONTACT JOINS	Small area from each part touches.	Ball to flat, Tube to flat, Rod to flat, Rod to rod	**POINT-OF-CONTACT JOINS** One Solder Point

of pipes installed by a power company or plumbing contractor. It is important to purchase the correct torch, hoses, regulator, and nozzles for the fuel system: they are not interchangeable.

Choosing a torch system appropriate to the work that will be made is one of the most difficult decisions an aspiring metals artist must make. The determining factors in purchasing a torch are how much heat is needed to do the intended work, combined with how much torch experience is needed to control that heat. Often artists first acquire a simple, small hand-held system, then later transition to a larger, portable propane or **MAPP gas** plumber's torch. After several years of experience in

making work, many finally upgrade to a mixed-gas unit. Whatever system you choose, you will follow a similar series of steps in making every solder join. The overall best practice when soldering is to keep the time the solder is under the torch as short as possible. This will preserve the integrity of the flux, the metal, and the solder and create a strong, stable, and aesthetically superior join.

PREHEAT THE ENTIRE WORK. Once the parts are set up and fluxed, the solder is positioned, and the quench bath is ready, light the torch. Then, hold the torch in your nondominant hand. Move the torch in a circular path, around the perimeter of the parts to heat the soldering block and the edges of

the metal. Continue the circular movement while observing the flux. Once the flux becomes glassy, it is time to focus closely on the solder join. *(Fig. 1)*

APPLY FOCUSED HEAT TO THE JOIN. Continuing to use a circular motion, move the flame of the torch directly to the join. Continue to heat the entire piece occasionally, but remain focused and moving along the seam as you observe the solder. It will first collapse under the heat of the flame and then flow. As soon as the solder begins to flow easily, use the torch flame to direct it along the join. Ideally, you will have positioned pallions to enter into the flow as the torch flame travels along the join. *(Figs. 2 & 3)*

WITHDRAW THE FLAME. When the solder has filled the join completely, keep the torch flame on the join for a second or less beyond that point, then remove it. Turn off the torch and place it on a fireproof surface. Quench the work in clean, clear, room-temperature water if desired; otherwise, allow it to cool on the soldering block before pickling. *(Fig. 4)*

Stage 3: Removing surface oxides, flux, and soils with pickle

Once you have soldered a piece, it is customary to quench the still-hot work in clean, clear, room-temperature water. Quenching directly in the pickle solution can damage the surrounding work area with splashes of the acidic solution and create excessive surface corrosion of the metal. Do not leave metal pieces in the pickle for any longer than it takes to remove the surface oxides.

Metal pickle is a diluted acid solution that chemically removes **firescale** from the surface and some **firestain** from just below the metal surface. It also removes flux, soil, carbon, and other materials that form on the surface of metal as it is heated during annealing, soldering, casting, fusing, and other techniques. Many types of acid can be used for the pickle bath, but the most common— and safest—are granulated, commercially prepared acids that are added to warm water in a lidded pickle pot.

Some pickle works best warm, others at room temperature: follow the manufacturer's directions to mix and prepare the solution. Always add acid to water. For granulated pickles, mix the granules into a small jar of warm water and stir them with a wood or glass rod until dissolved. Add this solution to the heated water in the pickle pot and mix well. Pickle should not be heated to more than 180°F (82°C) (pickle pots are set to this temperature). Also, never let the solution boil or let the pickle pot go dry or you will damage the pot. Pickle will become bright

Pickle pot

Copper tongs

Powdered acid granules

blue and saturated or spent. To neutralize spent pickle, cool it and mix baking soda into the solution. Then dispose of the copper-rich solution according to local chemical recycling regulations.

1. Leave the piece in the bath only as long as needed to remove visible oxides. In a warm solution, this is typically 1 to 4 minutes.

2. Remove the pickled metalwork with copper tongs and rinse thoroughly in clear running water. When removing or adding work to the pickle bath, it is important to use copper tongs: the presence of steel or iron will cause any copper ions in the pickle solution to adhere to the surface of whatever metal is in the bath at the time, and copper plating of all of the work will occur. Be sure to remove all steel or iron binding wire after quenching hot metal to avoid copper plating during pickling. Use a scratch brush to remove lingering soils (a toothbrush or small scrub brush and soapy water are also useful). Rinse the work and dry it completely before working on it with steel tools to prevent rust from forming on the tools.

Types of Soldering Methods

Method	Description	Applications
CHIP SOLDERING	Small sections of sheet or wire solder are cut and positioned along the join.	*The most common soldering method, good for every type of join.*
SWEAT SOLDERING	Solder is pre-melted on the back surface of a unit; the work is partially cooled, positioned, and the torch is reapplied. Also called **tinning**.	*For overlap joins, overlays, very large work, or difficult joins where control of solder flow is essential.*
PICK SOLDERING	Solder is cut and the torch is used to draw it into balls. A fluxed, pointed probe is used to pick up the heated ball and position it on the heated join.	*Useful for intricate or delicate work, as well as repetitive soldering operations, like chain making.*
PASTE SOLDERING	Commercially prepared grades of solder are sold, premixed with flux, in tubes. The mud is applied sparingly to the join.	*For filigree, delicate, or thin work, and for difficult-to-reach joins.*
STICK SOLDERING	Wire solder is held in tweezers and touched briefly to the heated join only at the moment the flux indicates the correct melting temperature.	*For repetitive soldering operations and production work. Takes control to master, as excess solder can flood the work.*
POWDER SOLDERING	Commercially prepared solder powders are available in several metal alloys and grades and are sprinkled on fluxed work.	*For filigree and other specialty techniques.*

APPLIED TECHNIQUE:
Four-Pendant Series with Four Different Solder Joins

This challenging series of four pendants focuses on the different types of solder joins: all will expose you to nearly every type of soldering operation and setup.

PENDANT ONE:
Two-metal sweat-soldered pendant with overlays (flat-on-flat)

1. Cut the overlays from 24-gauge brass and cut the backplate from 24-gauge nickel. Form the brass wire to extend past the end of the leaf for the bail and use a file or hammer and steel bench block to flatten the back of the annealed wire slightly. **Pickle and clean all parts:** check work fit.

2. Apply flux to both sides of all parts. Sweat hard solder on the backs of the overlays and wire. Let them cool briefly and position them on the nickel backplate. Heat work until solder reflows and parts are joined.

3. **Quench:** pickle, rinse, and clean-finish. Add a jump ring to the coiled loop if desired.

The easiest in the series, this pendant features flat-on-flat solder joins.

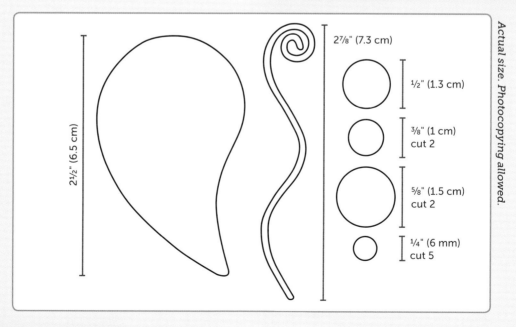

2⅞" (7.3 cm)

2½" (6.5 cm)

½" (1.3 cm)

⅜" (1 cm)
cut 2

⅝" (1.5 cm)
cut 2

¼" (6 mm)
cut 5

Actual size. Photocopying allowed.

Edge-to-edge solder joins are more difficult. Prepare the soldering block carefully to prevent gaps in the joins or misplaced elements.

PENDANT TWO:

Three-metal drilled and pierced pendant with butt-joined tubing inserts (edge-to-edge)

1. Cut the backplate from nickel. Drill and/or saw openings slightly smaller than the diameters of five graduated sizes of brass tubing: 3/8" (1 cm), 5/16" (10 mm), 1/4" (6 mm), 5/32" (5 mm), and 1/8" (3 mm).

2. File the openings carefully to allow the tubing to just fit inside: any looser than a tight fit will prevent a good join during soldering. Cut the tubing into 2 mm sections, one for each correspondingly sized opening.

3. Apply flux to all parts. Position backplate on 2 sections of binding wire to elevate it evenly above the surface of the solder block. Insert tubing into openings and position wire on surface. Cut pallions of solder and place them around the perimeter of the tubing (close, but not touching): also place several pallions along the wire.

4. Carefully heat the work. When the piece reaches soldering temperature, coax the solder into the seams and along the wire with the torch flame. Quench work after joining all sections of the tubing.

5. Pickle, rinse, and clean-finish. File a flat area on a 1/4" (6 mm) section of 3/8" (1 cm) tubing. Solder this on the back of the work to create a bail.

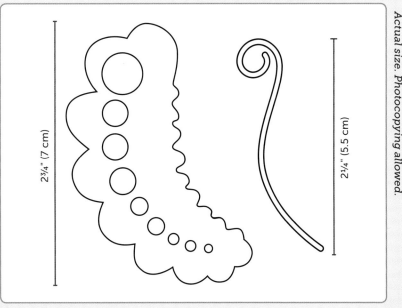

2 3/4" (7 cm)

2 1/4" (5.5 cm)

Actual size. Photocopying allowed.

PENDANT THREE:
Two-metal lap-joined pendant (sleeve overlaps)

1. Cut out the 24-gauge brass and copper leaflet units and saw-pierce their openings. Sand and finish all edges.

2. Coil the 14-gauge brass stem wire and gently form it into a graceful taper.

3. File a U-shaped depression in one end of the wire. Then form the stem wire into a D-shape for the bail on one end. File the other end to a taper. Clean-finish the wire and pickle it.

4. With round-nose pliers, gently bend each leaflet into a U-shape, matching the diameter of the U bend to the gauge of the stem wire. A tight fit is essential.

5. Flux all of the units on all sides and set them in order on the soldering table. Position the innermost leaflet on the fluxed stem wire and solder it in place. In the same operation, solder the D-bend of the stem wire closed. Quench the work in water, but do not pickle yet. Solder on the next two leaflets in order, in the same way, focusing the torch on the thick stem wire to avoid melting the leaflets. Pickle after groups of 3 leaflets are soldered in place, brass brush and clean the work, reflux it, and continue soldering the leaflets on, one at a time, pickling after 3 have been added. Vary the size and the metal colors down the stem wire.

6. Pickle the work well, rinse, and clean-finish, patinate as desired and then bring the raised areas of the piece to a high polish with rouge on a hard felt buff.

Soldered sleeve overlaps combine thin sheet with thicker wire. Control the flame to prevent thin parts from overheating on the soldering block.

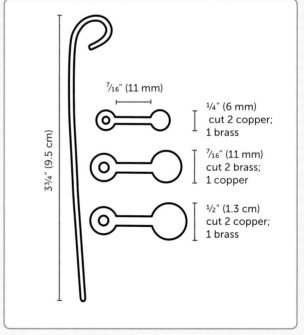

3¾" (9.5 cm)

⁷⁄₁₆" (11 mm)

¼" (6 mm) cut 2 copper; 1 brass

⁷⁄₁₆" (11 mm) cut 2 brass; 1 copper

½" (1.3 cm) cut 2 copper; 1 brass

Photocopy at 125%

PENDANT FOUR:

Three-metal pendant with point-of-contact solder joins (round-to-round and round-to-flat)

1. Cut out the 22-gauge copper backplate according to the pattern.

2. Cut lengths of 16-gauge brass wire and sand the ends of each section for the veins and central vein of the leaf. (Refer to the pendant photo and choose the number and lengths of wire you prefer.)

3. Using scraps of fine or sterling silver, heat and ball up enough well-formed, spherical granules of metal to equal 3 times the number of vein wires. Let cool. Pickle and rinse well. Set aside to dry.

4. Create a jump ring from a small section of 22-gauge sterling silver wire.

5. Flux the backplate and place it on a very clean firebrick. Solder on the central vein using very tiny chips of easy solder. Quench, pickle, rinse, and scrub well with warm soapy water. Inspect the seam and sand off any errant solder. There should be no visible solder along the copper.

6. Cover the entire surface of the backplate with flux. Position the first vein and solder it on with easy solder. Allow the work to cool, but do not quench or pickle. Keep adding vein wires and work down the leaf, until they have all been added. Pickle the piece well and scrub with a brass brush. Sand off any errant solder and clean-finish the work.

7. Draw marker lines parallel with the veins and center-punch a row of divots along each vein for drilling.

8. Carefully drill all the holes with a #59 drill bit. Go back and drill larger holes in the outer openings with a #51 drill bit. Finally, drill the outside holes with a #46 drill bit to create rows of graduated holes. Sand the piece on both front and back to remove burrs, then use a flame or bud bur to ream out the edges of the drilled holes gently.

9. Return the piece to the soldering brick and flux well. Use sharp tweezers to position the fluxed silver granules at the tip of each wire in grouped triangle formations. Then, position a small chip of easy solder in the center of each triangle group. Solder the granules down. Quench.

10. Pickle the work, sand, and clean-finish. Polish with Tripoli, patinate one side of the leaf, and polish a final time with jeweler's rouge.

Round-to-round metal parts and round-to-flat metal parts present a soldering challenge in both their placement and mass. To avoid overheating this piece, control the torch flame, sequence the joins correctly, and set up the parts carefully.

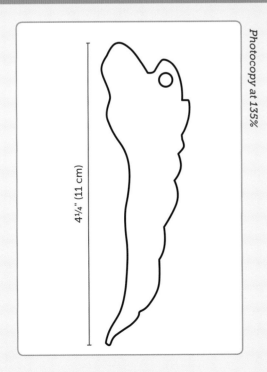

4¼" (11 cm)

Photocopy at 135%

PART FIVE:
Moving Metal

BUILDING BLOCK SEVEN:
Surface Texture and Embellishment on Flat Sheet

TOOLS USED IN THIS SECTION:
Rolling mill, texture hammers, metal stamps, anvils, bench blocks

CROSS-REFERENCES:
Material Preparation, *page 31*
Annealing Metal, *page 80*
Patination, *page 80*
Simple Metal Forming and Forging, *page 105*

The play of light over a highly polished metal surface is a feast for the eyes. A classic reflective and brilliantly polished metal surface is something every metals artist tries to perfect, especially when making jewelry for the purpose of selling it.

Customers favor shine, and the majority of jewelry consumers expect metal to be smooth and brilliantly polished. However, textured surfaces—particularly when used in tandem with the highly reflective ones—can add visual excitement to jewelry.

You can texture sheet metal in unlimited ways, both by hand and using specialized equipment. Hammers, punches, and stamps can be used to create **direct textures** on the metal surface; other methods, like embossing, can be used to create **transferred textures** on metal. Either way, metal surface texture, combined with the judicious use of **patination**, makes for appealing and attractive jewelry. Perhaps the most interesting way to create texture on metal is with a **rolling mill**, one of the "Holy Grail" tools of the workshop. Mills are heavy, costly, and a major investment; but once you own one, you will wonder how you ever functioned without it.

Flat stock vs. forming

When you strike metal with a hammer, the metal moves down and away from the point of impact because of the malleability of the material. Learning how specific metals will react when struck takes time and practice. One of the most important things to remember when texturing the surface of flat sheet is to work with steel backing the jewelry metal to prevent **deformation**, a natural result of metal malleability. Well-annealed metal is soft: an inflexible steel bench block, anvil, or other supportive steel surface reduces the metal's curl upward toward the hammer face as the metal is struck. This is the difference between **surface texturing** on flat stock, which can then be sawn and fabricated into 3-D objects *after* texturing it, and **metal-forming**, which creates 3-D forms *as it is hammered* through purposeful deformation of the metal and use of specially shaped stakes and hammer faces.

Direct textures

HAMMERS are available for many jewelry-making and metalworking purposes. In addition to a general-purpose hammer, there are specialized hammers made for forming, chasing, riveting, and direct-texturing. Basically, there are two broad categories of hammers: those that are designed to strike tools, and those that strike jewelry metal: do not mix them up. It is important to protect the faces of hammers made for striking metal, because any scratch, dent, pockmark, or scrape will transfer from the damaged hammer face onto the jewelry metal *on every hammer strike*.

FORMING HAMMERS can be used to form metal and texture flat sheet. They typically have polished faces, are curved and smooth, and many are heavy and large. There are several major categories of forming hammers that create pleasing surface texture on flat sheet: embossing and cross-peen hammers will make dimpled or lined surfaces and create highly polished marks in the depressions made where they impact the sheet.

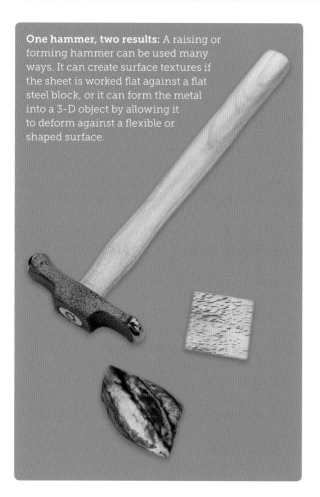

One hammer, two results: A raising or forming hammer can be used many ways. It can create surface textures if the sheet is worked flat against a flat steel block, or it can form the metal into a 3-D object by allowing it to deform against a flexible or shaped surface.

Direct texturing tools

Texture hammer, custom ground

Texture hammer with interchangeable heads

TEXTURE HAMMERS feature cut, carved, or other designs on their faces. The designs transfer to the sheet as the hammer strikes the metal. A wide selection of hammers is manufactured commercially: some have interchangeable faces. Custom-made hammers can be crafted by recycling old, inexpensive, or discarded hammers; annealing the steel; and then carving into it with files, a grinder, or other tools to create a textured surface. After that, the carved hammer head is **tempered** to return hardness to the steel before use.

Metal **STAMPS** and **PUNCHES** are struck with a chasing hammer, ball-peen hammer, or brass mallet. The pattern or design on the punch impresses directly into the metal. Most metal stamps are called "**single-blow punches**," because ideally the punch is struck once with the hammer to make the mark on the sheet. There are both decorative and nondecorative metal punches. Hallmark and quality-mark punches and stamps fall into the latter category. Handmade stamps and punches can be created from nails, steel rod, discarded chisels, files,

screwdrivers, and other steel tools in the same way that custom-textured hammer faces can be made.

Other direct-texture tools include **abrasive compounds** applied by power or hand, like sandpaper, aluminum, and silicon carbide, or diamond burs and bits for the flex shaft. Hand tools designed for scraping, carving, or cutting metal surfaces include scribes, triangle scrapers, and gravers: all of them can be used to create exciting surface textures.

Direct texturing tools (con't.)

Metal design stamps

Adapted screwdriver

Adapted cold chisels

Construction nails

Handmade stamping tools

Transferred textures

Plain sheet metal is created in an industrial mill by roll forming—a continuous process whereby a strip of metal is formed in sets of rollers to a desired gauge. Roll forming is used to produce long lengths of sheet or large quantities of parts. When the metal surface is textured but not directly struck or cut with a metal tool, the process is referred to as a **transferred texture**. Most often, these textures are achieved by an individual artisan who uses a rolling mill or a hydraulic press, both of which **emboss** the pattern or texture into the metal surface under great pressure. The rolling mill is the more commonly used tool in a small shop, although the hydraulic press has become more readily available for private studio jewelry workshops.

ROLLING MILLS are an important tool for every workshop. They can be used to reduce the thickness of ingots and sheet and to reduce the dimension of wire. Rolling mills also allow one to transfer texture to other metals. The rolls of a mill must be parallel, and each pass of the metal through the gap between them will reduce the total thickness or gauge of the sheet, while at the same time the length and width of the sheet spread are increased. Patterned rollers are available for some older mills, which produce consistent rolled textures similar to Florentine finishes, some floral patterns, and other designs.

CORRUGATION MILLS are specialty rolling mills that create undulating folds or waves on very thin-gauge sheet. Some models create waves of varying dimensions. Exciting patterns can be created with corrugated sheet that has been passed through a mill in several directions. Corrugated metal is often used in tandem with a hydraulic press to create hollow, die-formed objects that are textured with corrugated waves and lines that are also stretched or compressed by the die contours.

Transferred texturing tools

Interchangeable rolling mill rollers, crosscut patterns

Corrugation mill

Brass sheet metal embossing plates

Tube-wringer

Hydraulic press dies

DROP HAMMERS and STAMPING PRESSES have been in use in manufacturing since the industrial revolution, and small-scale HYDRAULIC PRESSES have recently become available for small-scale metal shops. Presses are specifically designed to perform one or two tasks, but all of them use compression or impact to transfer designs onto metal by impression stamping, shearing a blank or cut form, or embossing a relief design into the sheet. Modern presses work with many accessories, including dies and texture plates.

Types of Dies

Dies are steel tools used to cut or shape material using a press. Much like molds, they are often customized for the object that they create. In jewelry making, one- and two-part dies are used for several operations, with or without the aid of a press. Dies are named for their function.

BENDING DIES bend metal blanks at specific angles along a straight line.

BLANKING DIES produce a flat cutout of metal in a desired shape, and usually only outside contours and no internal cuts are made. The finished cutout is called a blank. These shapes are useful for production jewelers, because they are accurate, uniform, and flat. A disc cutter is a common type of blanking die.

BROACHING DIES are used to remove metal from thick edges of components that cannot be shaved. Shaving only removes a small amount of metal from edges to finish them.

BULGING DIES expand the end of tubes or other openings.

COINING DIES may be used to transfer designs or patterns on either face of the blank. The faces need not be identical.

CURLING DIES roll metal edges into a curved shape.

CUT-OFF DIES trim excess metal from a finished component.

DRAWING DIES are used to deform metal by extending around the sides of the form and pressing it inward and down.

EXTRUDING DIES severely deform metal blanks called **slugs** into components. Extreme pressure from the punch squeezes the metal into its final form.

FORMING DIES shape a blank along a specific curved line or surface. A dapping block is a common forming die.

HORNING DIES allow parts to be held or positioned for other pressings.

PANCAKE DIES are used for simple blanking and/or piercing on individual parts by hand.

PROGRESSIVE DIES modify the object over the course of several pressings until the final, finished part is complete.

SIDE CAM DIES modify the vertical motion of the press and change it into horizontal or angular motion.

SWAGING or **NECKING DIES** reduce the opening size on tubing or another component by compressing them inward.

TRIMMING DIES remove excess metal and are usually the last press operation performed.

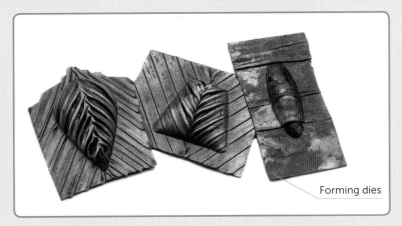

Forming dies

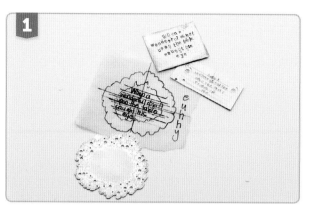

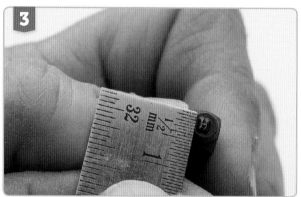

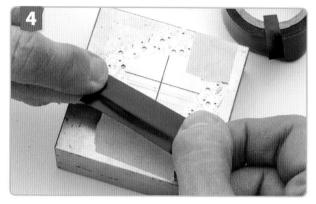

How to stamp metal evenly

It is well worth testing a handstamped text layout on practice metal to eliminate any potential problems. Take the time to doublecheck the placement and orientation of each stamp and correct spelling of the words. If you plan your design well and work slowly, it will be easy for you to stamp straight and clearly. To center lettering, the following method (which I learned in my art school typography class) works very well for metals.

1. Plan the layout of the text. Letter the word or phrase on a strip of paper to get an idea of what the letterforms will look like. Trace the perimeter of the metal and roughly letter the text with a pencil to prevent heartache in case words or phrases turn out to be too long. *(Fig. 1)*

2. Draw centering guidelines on the metal with a fine-line marker. Position the stamped text perpendicularly to make it easy to align with a small L-square and a machined steel block. Tape the metal to the block with masking or painter's tape. Draw a vertical line through the center of the metal and position the intersecting line at 90°—also in the center of the piece. Once you have located the center of the entire piece, creating lettering guides is easy. *(Fig. 2)*

3. For a single line of text, measure the depth of the lettering. Divide that measurement in half and draw a line at that measure, below the centerline. For example, using a 6 mm letter stamp, you would draw a second line 3 mm below the centerline. For multiline stampings, I generally space 1/16" (2 mm) between lines of text. *(Fig. 3)*

4. Lay a strip of electrical tape exactly along the line you drew. The tape will create a tiny "curb" against which to park the base of the letter on the stamp. Because all of the letters in a typeface are almost the same size, the tape will ensure aligned lettering. *(Fig. 4)*

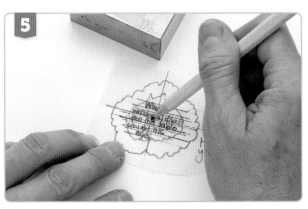

5. Count the number of characters in your word (or words). Spaces count as one character. In this example, the longest line is 14 characters. Divide the total character count in half (in this example, 7 and 7) to figure out which character gets stamped on the centerline. Make red marks in the center of each line of text and work from the center out, using the sketch as a guide. Cross off characters as you stamp them to avoid typographic errors. *(Fig. 5)*

6. Choose the center letter. Slide the stamp baseline down to meet the edge of the electrical tape. Take a peek to make sure the stamp is vertical, oriented correctly, and positioned against the tape. Strike once with the hammer. *(Fig. 6)*

7. Continue stamping using this method. I prefer to finish all of the letters on the right side of the centerline, then stamp all of the letters on the left side, but always working out from the center. Characters that descend below the baseline (in lowercase fonts) have to be positioned by eye, because the tape will prevent you from stamping a good impression, so take care. *(Fig. 7)*

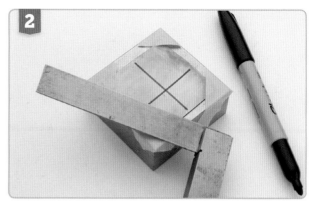

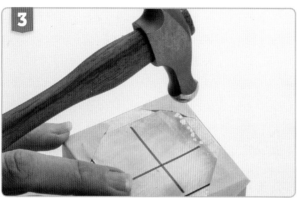

How to hammer an even texture

Developing eye–hand coordination will improve your ability to hammer an even allover texture. Working methodically across the sheet, practice using the same level of force for every hammer strike.

1. Metal ready for hammer texturing should be clean, oxide-free, annealed, and bone dry. Wet metal causes tool rust, and oxides on the metal will become embedded into the sheet during hammer texturing. *(Fig. 1)*

2. Place the sheet on a clean, flat, smooth steel block. Tape the four corners down with painter's tape or masking tape. Mark both a vertical and a horizontal line through the centers of the sheet. *(Fig. 2)*

3. Hammer across the sheet in one direction. Proceed across, creating an even row of marks. Use the drawn lines to guide your hammering; strive for even depth and even positioning of the strikes. *(Fig. 3)*

4. Proceed to the next row of marks and continue hammering. The hammered metal will work-harden, while the unhammered metal will remain annealed. Use this hammering method for any type of hammered texture. *(Fig. 4)*

Emboss with a rolling mill

Although a rolling mill is a large investment, it can be used for many purposes: embossing; reducing the gauge of metal sheet; transforming ingots into wire, rod, or sheet; and for milling square or round wire in specially grooved rollers. Each mill is different, but all should be treated with care.

1. Metal ready for the mill should be clean, oxide-free, annealed, and bone dry. Wet metal causes the rollers to rust, and oxides on the metal become embedded in the sheet when compressed, so they must be removed completely. Always pass the metal through the center of the rollers. Sandwich the source pattern within the metal to be printed: both the top and bottom sheets will be impressed by a two-sided object during roll printing. For single-sided roll prints, a copper or brass backing plate should be used to protect the rollers from damage. *(Fig. 1)*

2. Make a **dead pass**—one at exactly the gauge of the metal sandwich—with no attempt to reduce any thickness. Make a note of the measurement for the dead pass, using the roller gauge measurement dial. *(Fig. 2)*

3. The **roughing pass** is the first live pass through the gap in the mill. To make it, adjust the roller gears to reduce the gap one-quarter turn from the measurement determined during the dead pass. Check the evenness of the metal as it exits the rollers and try not to disrupt the pattern source if another pass is needed. *(Fig. 3)*

4. Most embossed patterns are made with one or two passes at most. Reduce the gears one-quarter turn for each live pass. For reducing the thickness of unpatterned sheet, the metal type and its thickness will determine the maximum amount of rolling. Usually, three or four passes are the maximum reduction before the metal needs to be annealed. Work-hardening will cause rolled metal to split horizontally; but do not anneal before the final pass if the metal is to be sawn. *(Fig. 4)*

APPLIED TECHNIQUE:
Wire Inlay between Roll-Patterned Metal Sheet

1. Roll-print several different patterns onto annealed 20- to 24-gauge sterling sheet. Following the pattern, saw out 10 overlays. Test the fit to ensure the channels between the overlays are evenly spaced and file as needed for uniformity.

2. Sweat-solder the patterned overlays to the 20-gauge bronze backplate with hard solder. Let the piece cool on the block, check the joins, pickle well, rinse, and dry. Use a knife-edge bur to slightly undercut the channels between the overlays so they are wider at the bottom where they rest on the backplate, than at the top opening.

3. Sweat-solder the sterling top circle overlay to the brass middle overlay. Quench, pickle, rinse, and finish to Tripoli pre-polish. Set assembly aside.

4. Anneal the 12-gauge copper and brass wires. Quench, pickle, rinse, dry, and polish. Flatten the wires by one-third of their thickness in the rolling mill, anneal: quench, pickle, rinse, and dry them again. Insert the wire into the channels, and hammer it into position by tapping it down at intervals with the flat peen of a goldsmith's hammer, a riveting hammer, or with a smooth chasing or setting punch and a chasing hammer. No soldering is needed once the wire has been compressed properly into the channel in the mill.

5. Sweat-solder the center overlay into position with medium solder.

6. Saw the perimeter of the piece cleanly, file and sand the edges, and patinate and polish as desired. For a pin, solder findings on the back; for a pendant, saw out one of the circular areas of the backplate, matching the edges of the circle on the silver overlay.

This challenging project allows you to use up small texture sample scraps. To avoid the potential of flooding the textured overlays with solder, anneal the wires between them and hold them in position by hammering them down into channels with a punch.

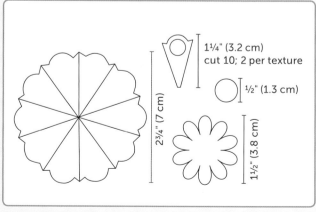

1¼" (3.2 cm)
cut 10; 2 per texture

½" (1.3 cm)

2¾" (7 cm)

1½" (3.8 cm)

Photocopy at 200%

DIRECT AND TRANSFERRED TEXTURES GALLERY

There are endless ways to texture sheet metal, limited only by the imagination or inventiveness of the jewelry maker. Once I create a sample texture I like, I document the texture method and punch a hole in the corner of the information card to attach it to the sample for easy reference. An alternate method is to create a 1" × 1" (2.5 × 2.5 cm) "charm" and drill it to attach to a jump ring. Attach the charm samples to a chain and write the texture method on the back of each with a marker.

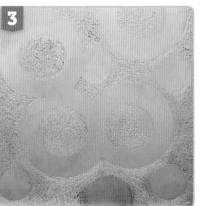

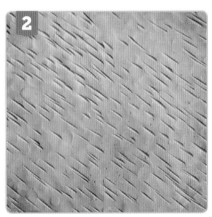

Direct textures

1. **One hammer, one direction:** Goldsmith's hammer, on the diagonal

2. **Two hammers, two directions:** Commercial texture hammer, allover; goldsmith's hammer, on the diagonal

3. **Diamond bur** within drawn outlines

4. **Allover dimpled texture** with embossing hammer

Direct textures (con't.)

5. **Two hammers, transitional pattern:** Chasing hammer, balled peen one edge; riveting hammer, cross-peen on opposite edge.

6. **Screwdriver–turned–metal stamp:** Planned pattern with allover design

7. **Stamped pattern combined with drilled hole.**

Transferred textures

8. **Commercially patterned brass plate** impressed into copper

9. **Hammered brass sheet–turned–printing plate:** Copper rolled against hammered brass

10. **Paper ribbon sandwiched between copper sheet:** Two passes with a 90° turn of the ribbon

11. **Window screen sandwiched between brass sheet and copper sheet**

12. **Feather sandwiched between copper sheet and brass sheet**

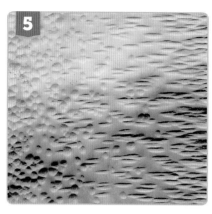

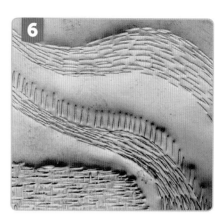

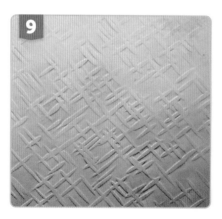

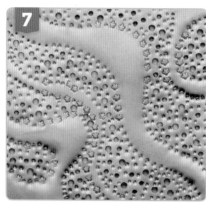

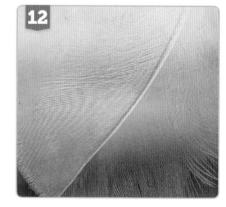

BUILDING BLOCK EIGHT:
Distorting Sheet Metal into 3-D Forms

TOOLS USED IN THIS SECTION:
Hammers, anvils, stakes,
blocks, mandrels, hydraulic press

CROSS-REFERENCES:
Material Preparation, *page 31*
Annealing Metal, *page 80*
Surface Texture and
Embellishment, *page 93*

Metalsmithing is all about the hammer. Hammering surfaces and fire are at the root of many smithing specialties: blacksmithing, silversmithing, and goldsmithing.

Even the root word of smith is related to the hammer—"to smite or strike." Flame, metal, anvil, and hammer is the purest and, to me, the most enjoyable way to work in this craft. Once you understand metal's plasticity, you can move it into fluid and sinuous shapes. The curved faces of hammers, shaped stakes, mandrels, and forming blocks can all be used to predictably "steer" the fluid, but solid molecules of metal into exciting forms—as long as you don't surpass the limits of a particular metal's plasticity. Metal in this stressed state—called **work-hardened**—is susceptible to cracking along its atomic structure lines because both the malleability and tensile strength of cold metal reduces with the impact of each successive blow. To reduce the built-up stress, metal must be annealed so the compressed molecules can expand once again; it returns to a state of soft plasticity.

Forging is the term used for moving metal by impact. Forging moves metal mass by repeated hammer blows and can be done on hot metal or cold, annealed metal. To differentiate between hot-forged metal (usually on ferrous iron and steel) and cold-forged metal (usually on nonferrous and precious metals), the terms forging and **forming** are used. Forging is hot; forming is cold.

Anvils and bench blocks: metal on

Flat or curved steel surfaces used to hammer metal on or against are commonly called **ANVILS**. The classic **horned anvil** is used as a hard surface against which to flatten, true up, and texture metal. They are available in a wide range of sizes. Large anvils are sold by weight; a good size for most jewelry-scale work is about 30 pounds (13.6 kg).

BENCH BLOCKS are portable steel squares or rectangles. They are invaluable for small-scale work such as riveting, flattening, and texturing. I keep several in my shop and often combine them: sandwiching annealed sheet between two very smooth blocks, then pounding with a mallet on the top block will flatten out a curve or warp. (Keeping the blocks' surfaces smooth is important so that marks and scratches don't transfer to your project metal when they are hammered.) Some **portable bench pins** include a built-in steel block.

CURVED and **DOMED ANVILS** are used to form larger metal domes and bowls. They come in several degrees of curvature and can be used as a surface against which to raise or texture, as well as a starting point for deeper metal-forming.

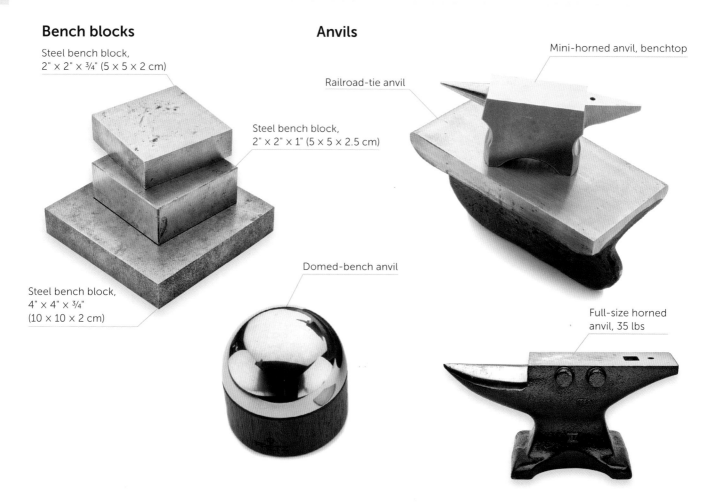

Bench blocks

Steel bench block,
2" × 2" × ¾" (5 × 5 × 2 cm)

Steel bench block,
2" × 2" × 1" (5 × 5 × 2.5 cm)

Steel bench block,
4" × 4" × ¾"
(10 × 10 × 2 cm)

Anvils

Mini-horned anvil, benchtop

Railroad-tie anvil

Domed-bench anvil

Full-size horned anvil, 35 lbs

Vises and mounts: metal held

Large-scale **BENCH-MOUNTED** or **SHOP VISES** are often used to hold other mandrels or anvils. However, they are also used to hold metal during folding or bending. Some vises have a flat surface, much like that of a bench block, to hammer on or against. It is important to mount a heavy vise to the worktop securely with carriage bolts to prevent injury. Many smiths mount both a vise and an anvil on a large section of tree stump to do their forming "in the round," meaning that they have access to the vise from all sides.

STAKE HOLDERS are a must when any stake with a **tang** is used for forming. For large silversmithing stakes, the often-tapered tang can be inserted into a corresponding **hardie hole** in an anvil, a feature present on most anvils larger than 20 pounds (9.1 kg). Micro-stakes must be used with the correct size stake holder, **vise mount**, or **stake support**.

EXTENSION ARMS are used in combination with an anvil or vise to allow the metalsmith to access an area of metal with a stake that may be difficult to position when inserted directly into an anvil or vise.

Vises and mounts

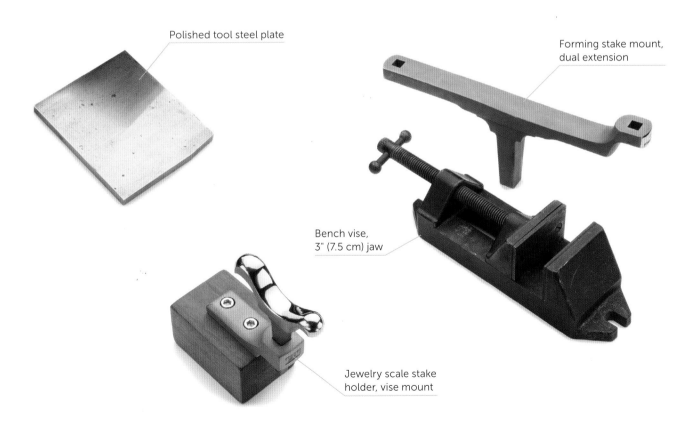

Polished tool steel plate

Forming stake mount, dual extension

Bench vise, 3" (7.5 cm) jaw

Jewelry scale stake holder, vise mount

Mandrels: metal around

All mandrels are rods or blocks of shaped steel, wood, or plastic and are designed to form metal against or around in specific, repeatable shapes.

BRACELET MANDRELS can be round or oval and stepped or tapered. Specialty bracelet mandrels feature highly polished surfaces, which should be protected to prevent marring; choose inexpensive versions to use for texturing metal. A **stepped bracelet mandrel** has specifically sized "steps" to prevent a taper from forming in a bangle bracelet; cuffs are formed on a tapered **mandrel** to conform to the shape of the arm. Many bracelet mandrels feature a tang at the base for insertion into a vise.

RING MANDRELS feature many of the same options as those for bracelets: stepped, tapered, and specially shaped, with the addition of ruled measurements for sizing, or not. Some ring mandrels are **grooved** to prevent damage to the **culet** of a gemstone ring, and newer shapes of mandrels include **square band** and **Eurostyle** (wider at the base for wearability).

NECKLACE MANDRELS are shaped like a bust. Made of highly polished steel, they can withstand repeated hammering and are designed for forming collars or wide, one-piece neck rings, or **torcs**.

BEZEL MANDRELS come in many of the more common shapes of faceted stones: round, triangle, square, octagon, pear, oval, and rectangle. They are very useful to create even, smooth stone settings. They are also used to work-harden soldered bezels prior to soldering them to a backplate by either using a rawhide mallet or, in the case of a round mandrel, rolling the bezel on a flat, hard surface with the bezel mounted on the mandrel.

Mandrels

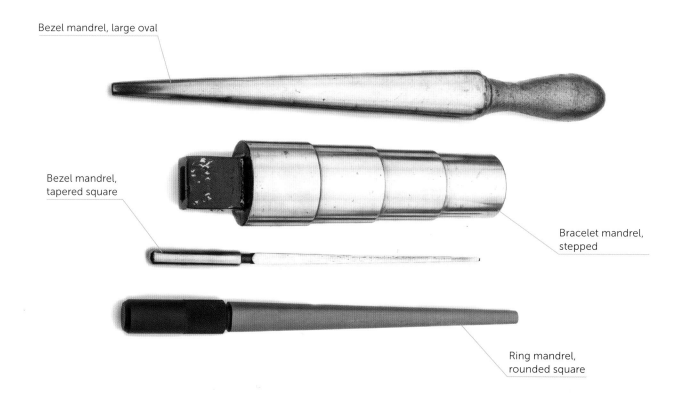

Bezel mandrel, large oval

Bezel mandrel, tapered square

Bracelet mandrel, stepped

Ring mandrel, rounded square

JUMP RING MANDRELS are very popular for creating **chain maille**, for production work, or for creating large quantities of jump rings or loops. Many can be inserted into a cranked **chuck** to speed production. A wide range of sizes is available.

Forming blocks: metal in

Forming blocks are used as a receptacle into which to force flat metal sheet. A corresponding punch or rod is used to impress the shaped blank of metal into the block. Daps and forming blocks are among the most simple tools used to move sheet into 3-D forms.

A **DAPPING BLOCK** combined with a corresponding **dapping punch** will create hemispherical or sometimes oval or spoon shapes from flat sheet-metal discs, either textured or untextured.

SWAGE BLOCKS are used to create grooves, troughs, tubes, and valleys with straight or curved sides. A corresponding rod is often used with a swage block, although a similar mandrel or hammer face can also move the metal into the groove of the block.

BEZEL BLOCKS and tapered **bezel punches** are used to shape stone settings in many commonly cut, calibrated shapes: round, oval, rectangle, square, and triangle are the most readily available from tool vendors.

DOMING BLOCKS are used to create shallow, bowl-like depressions in sheet. They are useful for creating large, shallow shapes as a starting point for hand-sinking or -raising.

Forming blocks

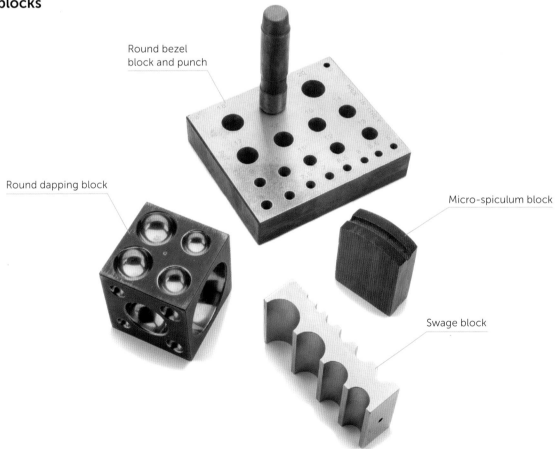

Round bezel block and punch

Round dapping block

Micro-spiculum block

Swage block

Hammers and forming and raising stakes: metal in and out and up and down

Stakes and hammers are used in tandem; to create bends, depressions, folds, or curves in sheet. A hammer and corresponding stake provide the impact and support for a developing form. The degree to which the metal will move when struck depends on several factors: the shape of the hammer peen, the material the hammer and the supporting surfaces are made from, and the force of the blow. There are hundreds of options when it comes to this class of tool; but they can be sorted roughly into basic groups. What you choose will depend on the final form of the metal you want to create.

HAMMER FACES come in several styles: flat, round, or convex; and in several shapes: oval, square, circle, rectangle. Typically, hammers are made with two differently shaped faces, or **peens/peins**. Mallets have identical peens. **Straight-peen hammers** have heads that are parallel to the shaft; **cross-peen hammers** have heads that are perpendicular to the shaft. Every hammer can be used on flat sheet to create surface texture. But when used for forming metal, hammers fit within the following categories:

RAISING HAMMERS feature highly polished faces that are oval or rectangular and wide in one direction and narrow in the other. They can be gently or severely curved, blunt, sharp, thick, thin, micro- or full-sized. All of them will create grooves, crimps, flutes, or depressions of various sizes when the metal is struck in combination with a supporting block, stake, or anvil. Raising hammers cause the metal to move at a *right angle to the strike*.

Forming hammers

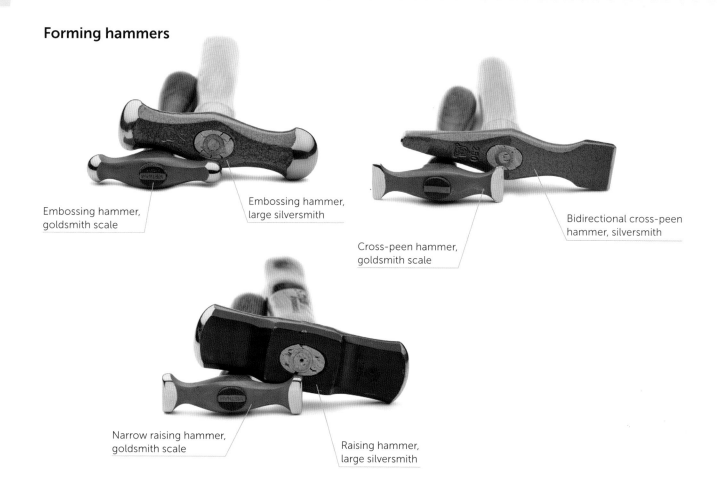

Embossing hammer, goldsmith scale

Embossing hammer, large silversmith

Cross-peen hammer, goldsmith scale

Bidirectional cross-peen hammer, silversmith

Narrow raising hammer, goldsmith scale

Raising hammer, large silversmith

EMBOSSING or **DOMING HAMMERS** have ball-shaped peens. They are used to create shallow and small depressions and cause the metal to move *away from the blow equally in all directions*. They are used for sinking, spotting, bottoming, and smoothing formed metal.

PLANISHING or **BOTTOMING HAMMERS** have both round and square faces. Typically, one face is slightly domed, or crowned, and the other is perfectly flat. It is critical to preserve the smoothness of a planishing hammer because it is intended to be used to *hand-polish the surface of an object by striking*

gentle blows. It requires great skill to use a planishing hammer well, as it must be struck on center or it will cause a dent, rather than erase one.

STAKES can be thought of as specialty anvils for forming. There are three types: T-stakes, which feature differently shaped working ends; one-arm stakes, which feature a single working end; and upright stakes, which extend straight up from the tang or holding projection of the stake.

T-STAKES are shaped like the letter T and include two working ends. They can be large for silversmithing,

or micro-sized for goldsmithing and are named for their traditional smithing functions: **bick irons**, bent and straight T-stakes, raising stakes, **blowhorns**, and **beakhorns**. Larger T-stakes are used for creating hollowware such as teapots, bowls, trophies, and serving ware. The working faces of all T-stakes are used as a surface against and around which to hammer metal and to create a standard repertoire of object forms: spouts, handles, bowls, and flutes. The micro-versions of these stakes echo these forms on jewelry-scale objects. T-stakes all feature a tang and are inserted into an anvil or holder during use.

Forming hammers (con't.)

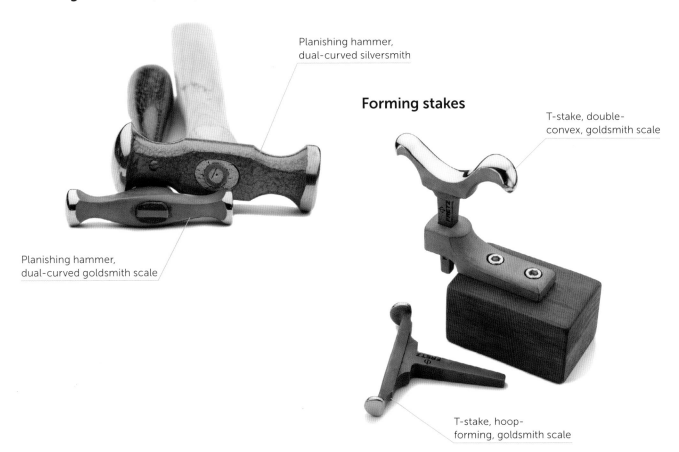

Planishing hammer, dual-curved silversmith

Planishing hammer, dual-curved goldsmith scale

Forming stakes

T-stake, double-convex, goldsmith scale

T-stake, hoop-forming, goldsmith scale

ONE-ARM STAKES are roughly L-shaped or straight. They include the **snarling iron**, **spout iron**, **handle iron**, and **sinusoidal stake**. All one-arm stakes are designed to reach far inside of closed or narrowly curved forms; the sinusoidal stake is used to raise anticlastic curves of varying size.

END-HOOK STAKES perform the same task but do not cause a twist in the hammered form. One-arm stakes are held in a specialty holder or bench vise during use.

UPRIGHT STAKES include mushroom, cone, anvil, domed, ball, hatchet, and fist-shaped heads which project straight up from the tang. They can be mounted in holders or in the hardie hole of an anvil. They are used

much like a shaped anvil; repeatable forms can be created on their faces, and they were traditionally used to

create flatware including spoons, forks, and knife handles. Micro- and full-sized versions are available, too.

SYNCLASTIC

One direction—
will hold water

Synclastic curves are simple and one-directional: they can be thought of as bowls or spheres.

ANTICLASTIC

Bi-directional—
will not hold water

Anticlastic curves are opposing and two-directional: they are saddle shaped.

Forming stakes (con't.)

One-arm stake, nylon shell forming

One-arm stake, sinusoidal

One-arm stake, large end hook

Upright stake, mushroom

Upright stake, flat cuff

Upright stake, flat mushroom

Utility hammers: alternative metal movers

Utility hammers are designed to strike other tools, such as stamps, punches, dies, and cutters. It is important to differentiate between highly polished forming hammers with flawless and beautifully polished faces versus plain ball-peen or other all-purpose hammers designed to strike tool steel. Although this class of tool can be used to strike and even move metal, they are not designed for that purpose.

BALL-PEEN, or machinist's, hammers are generalists in the metal shop; they are designed for all-purpose use with such techniques as stamping, chiseling, die-cutting, punching, and folding. Often, these inexpensive hammers can be custom-ground by the smith to perform specialty functions such as texturing.

MALLETS can be made of wood, hide, fiber, bamboo, plastic, rubber, brass or copper. They are used to move metal without deforming it. Mallets come in many sizes and weights and have two faces that are identically shaped; some are weighted on one side. **Dead-blow mallets** do not bounce or kick back when they are struck.

CHASING HAMMERS and corresponding punches are used to form metal on a micro-scale. The chasing hammer is designed to strike chasing punches and features a very flexible and thin wood handle that acts much like a whip when it strikes a chasing punch. The large peen is designed to find the striking end of a punch without your having to aim the hammer precisely—during chasing and repoussage, the eyes are focused on the tip of the punch, not the hammering. Chasing punches can be thought of as micro—hammer faces: they form the metal by pushing it instead of cutting it, just as a metal stamp would.

Utility hammers

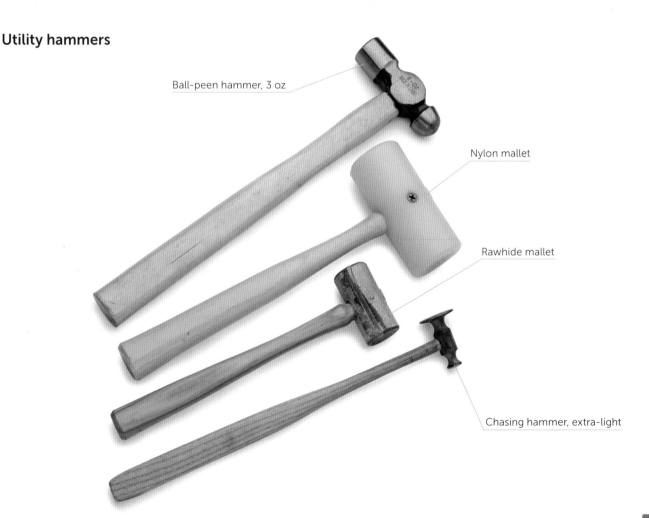

Ball-peen hammer, 3 oz

Nylon mallet

Rawhide mallet

Chasing hammer, extra-light

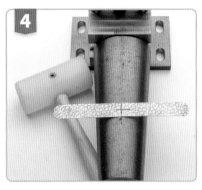

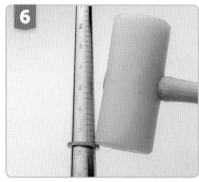

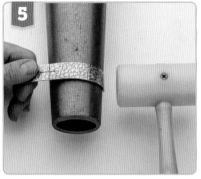

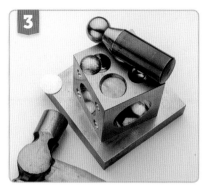

How to dap a hemisphere

Simple formed shapes like hemispheres are easy to create with a combination of a block and corresponding punch. Work with dry annealed metal for the best results.

1. Cut a disc of plain or textured metal with a saw or disc cutter. Insert the disc into the indent that most closely matches the outer diameter of the disc. Err on the side of a larger indent, and if the metal is textured, position the textured side up for a convex final design and down for a concave one. *(Fig. 1)*

2. Choose a dapping punch that is smaller than the diameter of the indent and that allows for the gauge of the metal. Ideally, the punch and the metal combined will equal the inner diameter of the indent. *(Fig. 2)*

3. Strike the punch evenly with a ball-peen or other utility hammer. Take care to hammer evenly and prevent the disc from sliding around in the indent. When the metal bottoms out, move it to the next smaller indent and punch combination, working in this way until the desired curvature is achieved. *(Fig. 3)*

How to use a bracelet or ring mandrel

The fabrication of many standard jewelry components and objects begins on a mandrel. Tapered mandrels allow a jewelry maker to size rings or bracelets up or down. Untapered mandrels make it possible to create a same-sized shape again and again.

1. Insert the mandrel into a vise, a holder, or the specially designed opening of a bench. Work with clean, dry, annealed metal. *(Fig. 4)*

2. Using a nylon mallet, hammer the ends of the stock inward first; only after hammering the ends in should the middle of the blank be formed. For a soldered band, focus on getting a good join at the seam, as the ring or bracelet can be rounded up again after soldering the join. *(Fig. 5)*

3. To size a ring up, hammer the edge of the band down to a larger diameter with the mandrel held vertically; after a few hammer strikes, flip the band on the mandrel and hammer again to prevent a taper from forming. *(Fig. 6)*

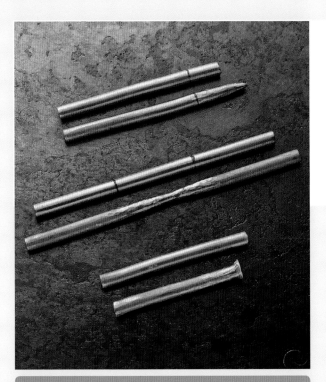

Practice metal-forming technique by changing the profile of stock metal rod through hammering.

APPLIED TECHNIQUE:
Hammer Tapers into Bar Stock

Three exercises to develop forming technique.

1. **Drawing down a rod:** Hammer a 2" (5 cm) long round, square, or rectangular 6-gauge rod with a cross-peen hammer, so the width of the rod does not change, but the length of the rod is increased. Do not allow a fishtail to form; the tapered end must transition smoothly to a point as shown. Planish the form smooth with a planishing hammer after forming.

2. **Setting down a rod:** Hammer a 4" (10 cm) long round 6-gauge rod with a cross-peen hammer, until the center inch (2.5 cm) of the rod is half the width of the ends of the rod and transitions smoothly. Planish the form as in the previous exercise.

3. **Upsetting a rod:** Hammer the edge of a 6-gauge rod to widen the gauge to a perfect circle 3-gauge wide. This must be done with the rod positioned vertically. Planish the form as above.

PART SIX:
Putting It All Together

BUILDING BLOCK NINE:
Stone Settings

TOOLS USED:
bezel rollers, bezel pushers, burnishers, beading tools, flex shaft, engraver's block, hand vise

CROSS-REFERENCES:
Jewelry Stones, *page 18*
Soldering, *page 83*

Once you have mastered the basics of fabrication, one of the most beautiful ways you can enhance a metalwork design is to add color to handmade jewelry in the form of set gemstones.

Gems earmarked for jewelry must be evaluated first for durability and wearability in accordance with the form o the final jewelry object. Rings and bracelets call for hard stones because the potential for damage is greater than for a brooch or necklace. After durability, color is probably the next most important factor to consider in a stone. Last, you can determine which style of stone setting or mount will best enhance the design of the piece and protect the stone. A stone setting not only holds a stone in position, it also protects against damage from impact. Settings fall into several categories, and each style has traditional applications.

Stone-setting tools

BEZEL ROLLERS, **ROCKERS**, or **PUSHERS** are used to compress the metal of the bezel collar against the stone in an orderly sequence. There are several shapes, styles, and sizes on the market, and most of them feature matte, rounded, or curved faces to prevent damage to the soft or fragile metals typically used to fabricate bezels.

PRONG PUSHERS are used to move prongs gently against the **girdle** of a stone. They have grooved faces and are typically mounted in a **graver**-style handle.

SETTING PUNCHES are used with a chasing hammer to compress a tube, gypsy, or channel setting against a stone. Steel punches can crack fragile stones, so you'll need to have several setting punches on hand in brass, copper, and steel to use according to the hardness of both the stone and the metal of the jewelry object.

BURNISHERS are used to polish and refine a bezel or tube setting that has been compressed against a stone. They can be made of steel or stone and are highly polished. Burnishers come in many styles: straight, curved, narrow, wide, short, or long. Handmade versions can be made from recycled toothbrush-handle plastic: this is the best tool to use for very soft stones, pearls, or shell.

BEZEL BLOCKS and **PUNCHES** are used to fabricate tapered bezels and basket settings in standard shapes such as oval, round, pear, triangle, or square. Corresponding punches match the profile of the openings in the block to create countless sizes of settings.

BEZEL-SETTING PUNCHES are tapered mandrels that feature a hemispherical indent on one end. They are inserted into a graver-like handle and used to burnish round settings once the stone has been mounted. It is important to keep the inner surfaces of these tools clean and highly polished so they won't mar the setting during fabrication.

Stone-setting tools

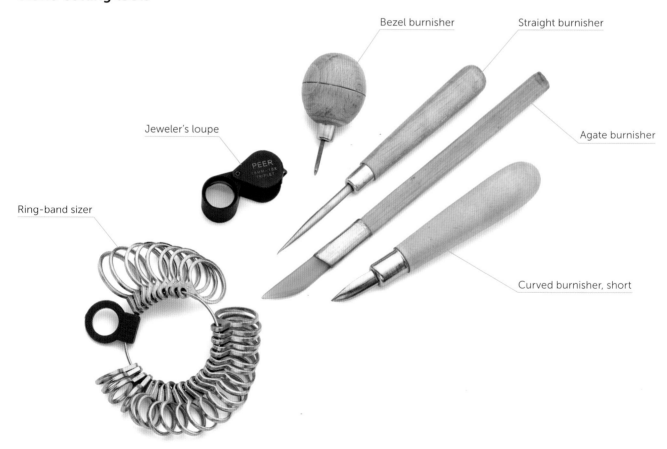

Ring-band sizer

Jeweler's loupe

Bezel burnisher

Straight burnisher

Agate burnisher

Curved burnisher, short

GRAVERS are invaluable for fabricating complex stone settings and settings that feature sharp angles. They can be used for minute refinements to **stone seats**, and a sharp graver can remove a tiny sliver of metal where no other tool can reach. Gravers are sharpened on an oilstone and must be sized to fit your hand.

BEADING TOOLS are used for bead settings and **pavé** settings and are available in graduated sets for creating many sizes of beads. They can also be used to texture the surface of metal without the use of stones. Beading tools dull quickly when used with hard metals: a beading block and sharpener will return them to their original state.

CLAMPS for stone setting can be bench-mounted or handheld. Often, they are secured in a vise or other holder to free both of your hands to work with the setting tools and the jewelry object. **Ring clamps**, **engraving balls**, and **setting sticks** are the tools most commonly used to hold jewelry during stone setting. Setting sticks and blocks are used in combination with a flexible holding medium such as **wax** or **thermoplastic**, which is removed after the stones are set. All clamps must be sturdy enough to withstand the great force needed to compress the setting against the stone.

Stone-setting tools (con't.)

Beading tool

Bezel rocker/roller

Prong pusher

Stone-setting categories

BEZEL or **RUB-OVER SETTINGS** are the oldest, most common, and most basic style of setting. Their construction typically includes an open or closed backplate and a soldered strip of plain or patterned metal called the bezel. A bezel can be thought of as a frame or collar with an inner opening that exactly matches the contour of the stone. Most bezels completely encircle the stone; some are partial. Bezels can be decorative or plain, thick or thin, but they are most commonly constructed out of soft metals such as fine silver or gold.

TUBE SETTINGS are fabricated from ready-made metal stock. The inner diameter of the tubing must be slightly smaller than the girdle diameter of the stone, and the outer diameter of the tube must be slightly larger than the diameter of the stone. A bur that matches the diameter of the stone is used to ream out a tapered seat so that approximately 0.4 mm (about 26-gauge) of metal remains to rub over the girdle and secure the stone.

GYPSY or **FLUSH SETTINGS** situate the stone so the top surface, or **TABLE**, is level with the metal surface. The thickness of the metal must match the depth of the stone, from table to the tip of the **CULET** or more. This style of setting is easiest to use on curved surfaces in harder metals. It is imperative that the seat be cut so the table of the stone is absolutely level with the surrounding metal surface.

CHANNEL SETTINGS feature a row of set stones that touch each other within two parallel grooves cut into the metal. The walls of metal holding the stones are burnished over all of the stones at the same time, once they have been set into the piece. It is important that the channels be level, at the proper depth to position the girdles of the stones consistently, and that enough metal remains to secure the stones firmly.

PRONG SETTINGS are typically used for transparent faceted stones with pointed backs. They are usually

Stone Settings

Bezel

Prong

Tube

Basket

Flush or Gypsy

Bead

Channel

Tension

lightweight and open to allow maximum light into the setting, but must be strong enough to secure the stone. Sometimes prong settings are closed in the back—usually for fragile or pale-colored materials—but, care must be taken with this kind of setting to prevent dirt and moisture from entering the space between the stone and the metal, which cloud the stone.

BASKET SETTINGS are named for their resemblance to woven baskets. They are open frameworks that include prongs and hold a stone securely, while allowing the maximum amount of light into the setting.

BEAD or **GRAIN SETTINGS** are created with a special tool. After burring out a seat the same diameter of the stone, fine splinters of metal called **GRAINS** or **SPURS** are cut with a half-round graver around the seat. Then, the stone is positioned and the grain is burnished and compressed into a ball shape with a beading tool so it will hold the stone. Beads can hold one or more stones simultaneously. This type of setting demands precision placement of the stone settings and beads and controlled burring with the flex shaft.

TENSION SETTINGS exploit the natural forces inherent in work-hardened metal to hold the stone in position without prongs. (When metal is work-hardened, it is very strong and resistant to movement.) This type of setting requires precise fabrication, and very hard metals are essential, both to protect the stone and to hold the stone with the force required. Often, stainless steel, white gold, platinum, or titanium is used for this type of setting.

COMBINATION SETTINGS feature construction methods derived from one or more other types of setting. Partial bezels can be combined with tube settings, prongs, or other styles of setting in limitless combinations.

Proper Bezel Heights

Every stone is unique. There is no rigid set of rules to follow when setting any individual stone, but a good guideline to remember is *the taller the stone, the taller the bezel*. It is important to create a bezel at just the right height to hold the stone securely, while at the same time not obscuring too much of it.

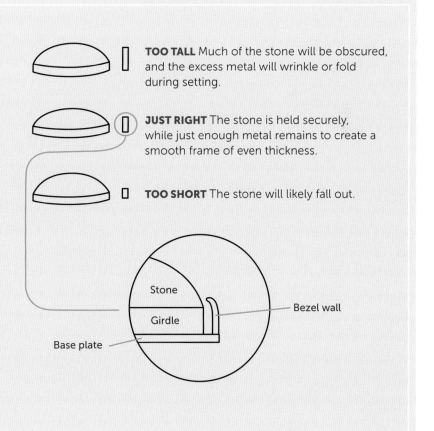

TOO TALL Much of the stone will be obscured, and the excess metal will wrinkle or fold during setting.

JUST RIGHT The stone is held securely, while just enough metal remains to create a smooth frame of even thickness.

TOO SHORT The stone will likely fall out.

Stone

Girdle

Base plate

Bezel wall

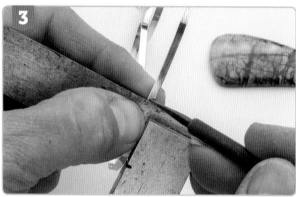

Making bezels that fit

Depending on the shape of a cabochon and how well it is cut, creating a bezel is one of the simplest and most beautiful ways to set a stone. Each stone is unique, but certain common factors make every individual bezel fabrication similar. Although bezels are the most popular and most oft-made style of setting, they are deceptively difficult to fit correctly. The most important fabrication step is patience: take the time to carefully measure and look at the bezel from every angle before soldering it closed. It is critical to file the cut edges so they are perpendicular to the backplate, straight, of even thickness, smooth, clean, and perfectly joined—all of which can be quite difficult to achieve on a very tiny piece of thin metal.

1. Set the stone on a flat surface. Wrap the bezel wire around the stone so that the wire is in contact with both the flat surface and the girdle of the stone. Encircle the stone completely until the bezel wire firmly overlaps. Ensure the wire is perfectly straight and that it stands perpendicular to the flat surface. *(Fig. 1)*

2. With a sharp scribe, mark a line at the place where the outer section of the overlapped wire just passes the cut edge of the inner wire. Remove the bezel from the stone. *(Fig. 2)*

3. Use an L-square to scribe a cutting line a hair's width past the mark to allow for sanding the cut edge. After cutting the bezel, sand to the marked line, true up the bezel wire, patiently bring the cut ends together into a perfect fit, and solder them closed with hard solder. *(Fig. 3)*

APPLIED TECHNIQUE:
Pendant with Three Differently Shaped Bezels

Fabricating three different bezels and combining them on a pendant is a great way to perfect your stone-setting skills. Careful and patient work will reward you with secure and beautiful settings for your gemstones.

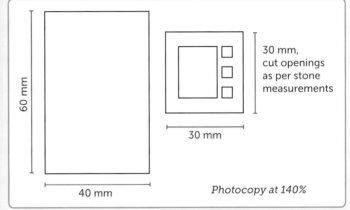

60 mm

40 mm

30 mm

30 mm, cut openings as per stone measurements

Photocopy at 140%

Set the oval stone first, then the other stones, and burnish the bezels to a high polish.

1. A round stone is the easiest shape for which to create a setting. Place the stone on a flat surface and wrap the bezel wire around the stone completely until the wire overlaps. Mark a line at the place where the outer section of the overlapped wire just passes the cut edge of the inner wire. Remove the bezel from the stone. Use an L-square to scribe the cutting line; cut and sand to the marked line. Fit the ends together and solder them closed with hard solder. Quench, pickle, rinse, and inspect the bezel for fit. If the bezel walls are too high, sand gently to the correct height. The stone should just

drop into the setting. Set aside. Create bezels for the oval and square stones in the same way.

2. When all 3 bezels have been created, fabricate the backplate from the pattern. Create a textured and pierced square overlay and cut the strip of wire. Sweat-solder both the overlay and wire to the backplate with hard solder. Bring everything to prepolish with Tripoli on a felt buff.

3. Fabricate the bail from a length of square brass tubing the same width as the backplate and solder it into position with medium solder. Quench, pickle, rinse, and clean up the pendant (file and/or sand) in preparation for soldering on the stone

bezels. Solder the bezels to the backplate with easy solder. Quench, pickle, and rinse the entire piece, clean everything well, and bring the entire pendant to a polish, then stamp the decorative border around the overlay. Scrub pendant well in warm soapy water, dry, and patinate the textured areas as desired.

4. Use a **separating disc** to cut a small slit in each of the corners of the square setting to allow it to be more easily set. Also use the disc to notch the slits in the side of the bezel to echo the design of the square cutouts on the overlay. File, sand, and clean up the pendant as needed. Do not neglect the finish on the outer edges and back of the work.

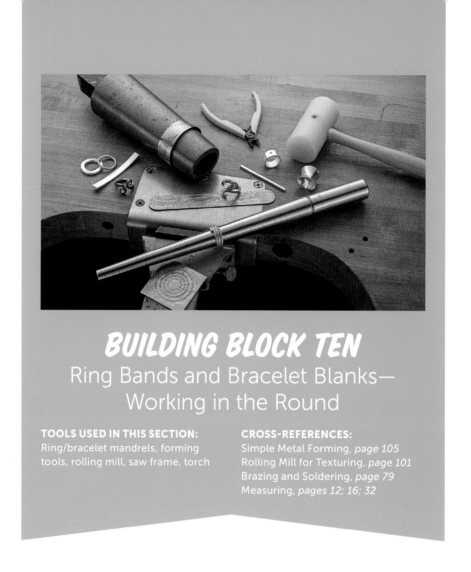

BUILDING BLOCK TEN
Ring Bands and Bracelet Blanks—
Working in the Round

TOOLS USED IN THIS SECTION:
Ring/bracelet mandrels, forming
tools, rolling mill, saw frame, torch

CROSS-REFERENCES:
Simple Metal Forming, *page 105*
Rolling Mill for Texturing, *page 101*
Brazing and Soldering, *page 79*
Measuring, *pages 12; 16; 32*

The human body is curved, and the most comfortable jewelry conforms to those curves. Creating rings or cuff and bangle bracelets that fit well is one of the greatest challenges in jewelry making.

Unlike a piece assembled from flat, linked units, a ring or cuff made of one continuous band of shaped metal is complex to plan and fabricate. But once you master the process for making these curved pieces, there is nothing more satisfying than getting a perfect fit. Smooth edges, fine finishing, and gentle transitions in the form are all important aspects when you design a pleasing ring or cuff. Plus, these jewelry objects receive more wear and tear than any other type, so you'll need to choose carefully which raw materials to use before fabrication begins.

Factors to consider when designing rings

Because the tolerances of an object as small as a ring are quite demanding, dozens of minute decisions must be made when creating one. It is no easy task to fabricate an object where the difference between a perfect fit and not can be as small as half a millimeter.

- For a ring to fit well, it must pass over the large knuckle of the finger comfortably, but be small enough to stay put once it has. Often, the large knuckle is two to three sizes bigger than the thinnest part of the finger base. For a thin band, sizing over the knuckle can be snug, but for a thick band, it must be close to the knuckle size or the ring will not easily come off the finger after wearing it for some time.

- A heavy stone or cluster of stones will cause a thin-banded ring to rotate—and the beautiful stones will decorate the palm rather than the front of the hand.

- The metal of the band must be of a thick enough gauge and any gemstones chosen must be durable enough to suffer the trials of everyday use.

- Take measurements of the finger several times over the course of a day to see if the size varies—often, fingers are fatter in the early hours of the day. Size a ring according to the average measure of the finger.

- Seasonal temperature/humidity change can affect ring sizes, too. In cold climates, finger size can drop by a full size, while during a hot or humid summer, finger size can increase by a size or more.

- Measure the length of the base of the finger starting about 3 mm above the uppermost point of the webbing between the fingers and stopping about 3 mm below the lowest fold of the large knuckle: this is the maximum width of a comfortable ring band for that finger.

Common ring band designs

Round band from half-round stock— This ring is a classic style and most often is the first soldered ring that an aspiring jewelry maker will fabricate. *(Fig. 1)*

Round band from round stock— For a clean solder join, this style is most easily made using a method similar to creating jump rings: coil the metal stock around a mandrel the same size or slightly smaller than the final size of the ring. *(Fig. 2)*

Bypass without stone—A nonsoldered ring that exploits the strength of work-hardening the metal during forming. The bypass can be horizontal, vertical, or diagonal. *(Fig. 3)*

1 ROUND; ½ ROUND

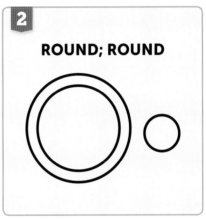

2 ROUND; ROUND

3 BYPASS; NO STONE

Bypass with stone—This style of ring shank is another classic design with thousands of options for adding many kinds of material. *(Fig. 4)*

Synclastic curve band—This dome style can be soldered to a flat metal band ring after forming it to create a very strong, but very light hollow object. The metal in the center of the curve is stretched, and the edges are compressed to create the dome. *(Fig. 5)*

Anticlastic curve band—This form must be stretched along the edges of the curve and compressed in the center, while at the same time, the curve of the ring band is created by pulling the narrow edges of the band toward each other to eventually solder closed. *(Fig. 6)*

Eurostyle—The Eurostyle band is a good choice for rings that feature heavy stones or settings. The band is wide at the base and narrow at the top to prevent slipping. It is a very comfortable style on the finger. *(Fig. 7)*

Square band—A square band is a good style for thicker gauge shanks or for wide metal. *(Fig. 8)*

4

BYPASS; WITH STONE

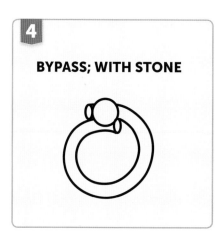

5

SYNCLASTIC DOME

6

ANTICLASTIC CURVE

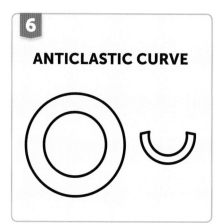

7

EUROSTYLE

8

SQUARE BAND

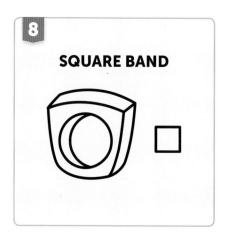

APPLIED TECHNIQUE:
Form a Bypass Ring Band

Thick wire and a forming hammer are the starting point for a fun-to-wear and fun-to-fabricate ring.

1. Cut a strip of 8-gauge square wire 85 mm long (for a size 8 ring). Clean-finish the cut ends of the metal and anneal, pickle, and rinse. Dry the metal completely.

2. Hammer a gentle taper in both ends of the wire, while maintaining the square profile, until the resulting gauge is about 12. The length of the strip will increase by about 20 mm.

3. Anneal the metal as needed, then planish the wire smooth with the curved face of a planishing hammer. After annealing prior to shaping on the ring mandrel, bring the surface of the tapered wire to a pre-polish.

4. With round-nose pliers, curl the tips of the wire into graceful loops, then position the annealed blank on a ring mandrel at the desired size.

5. Hammer the ring with a mallet into the final shape, taking care to bring the ends in evenly and not deforming the curled ends during shaping.

APPLIED TECHNIQUE:
Hammer an Anticlastic Curve into a Ring Band

1. Cut the pattern out of 20-gauge sterling sheet as shown (for a size 8.5 band). Clean-finish the cut ends of the metal and anneal: quench, pickle, and rinse. Dry the metal completely.

2. Position the ring blank in the bay of a **sinusoidal stake** or in an **end-hook stake** so the blank fits into the depression without touching the bottom of the curve.

3. With the cross-peen of a narrow plastic or nylon mallet, hammer the edges of the blank evenly along its length to stretch the metal and cause it to meet the curvature of the stake. At the same time, hold the narrow ends of the ring blank to cause the ring to round as the metal is hammered. Anneal as needed.

4. Once the desired curvature is achieved, use a jeweler's saw to cut straight edges on both narrow ends of the blank, where you will next solder it closed. The ring will stretch as it is formed, so after forming, metal must be removed to reduce the blank to the correct size. Alternatively, leave the band unsoldered.

The understated beauty of a simple curved strip of silver is easy to create once you understand the differently shaped curves created by metal forming.

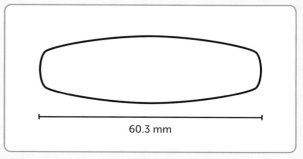

60.3 mm

Actual size.

APPLIED TECHNIQUE:
Texture and Form a Tapered Cuff Bracelet

1. Choose a texture source and roll-print the blank or hand-texture a design by hammering or stamping the metal. Taping the metal blank to a bench block with blue painter's tape will hold the metal steady during hand texturing.

2. Cut the pattern out of 18-gauge sterling or copper sheet. File, sand, and clean-finish the cut ends of the metal and anneal: quench, pickle, and rinse. Dry the metal completely.

3. Anneal the textured metal. Quench, pickle, rinse, and dry the metal completely.

4. Make a mark on the bracelet mandrel at the desired size. With a rawhide mallet, hammer the ends of the band together, taking care not to distort the pattern during forming.

Cuffs are a great way to show off an interesting metal texture—whether it is created by a direct or transferred technique.

5⅞" (15 cm)

Actual size.

TIP: *For a cuff that measures wider than 1" (2.5 cm), allow the opening to form a narrow V that conforms to the taper of the arm for comfort when wearing.*

BUILDING BLOCK ELEVEN:
Links and Units—Chains, Bands, and Linkage Systems

TOOLS USED IN THIS SECTION:
Ring/bracelet mandrels, forming tools, rolling mill, saw frame, torch,

CROSS-REFERENCES:
Mandrels, *pages 108; 114*
Piercing and Separating, *page 47*
Brazing and Soldering, *page 79*
Measuring, *pages 12; 16; 32*

Very often, aspiring jewelry makers enter the craft by way of **unit construction**—they purchase manufactured metal components at a craft or hobby store, then connect them using soldered or unsoldered jump rings or by some other method.

After learning fabrication techniques, they can custom-create rather than purchase these metal units. The simplest unit of jewelry linking systems consists of a plain ring of unsoldered wire—the jump ring, while the most elaborate unit can be a complex gemstone-encrusted, saw-pierced medallion or link as decorative or plain as the designer wishes. Regardless of the design of a particular unit, connecting and assembling like or dissimilar units into a flexible, linear section of links is as old as the craft of jewelry making itself.

CHAIN is one of the oldest forms of jewelry. As early as 3500 BC, ancient goldsmiths used thin, hand-hammered ribbons of gold to create chain, which was interworked or linked. **Interworked chain** is made from one continuous length of wire. **Linked chain** is made of narrow, linear sections of individual units, which may be unsoldered or joined by soldering. Those units can be called links, rings, or loops and can be identically sized and shaped or not. The process of joining the links is sometimes called **chain weaving**. When the links form larger, flexible swaths of fabriclike interlocked rings, they are called **chain maille** (or chain mail).

FINDINGS are functional parts that can be fabricated or purchased. Findings can link parts of a jewelry object to other parts of the object, or to the body or clothing of the wearer. Findings include clasps, pin stems, jump rings, head pins, ball pins, eye pins, earring posts, earring wires, caps, sleeves, cones, up eyes, fasteners, clips, key rings, and bails.

Types of Chain

BOX CHAIN is a simple chain made with square links.

FLAT CHAIN has an obvious front and back, and the rings or links lie in a specific direction.

LINK-AND-PLATE CHAIN connects metal shapes within a repeat of rings or links.

PADDLE CHAIN features long flat links connected with small round rings or links.

REPEAT CHAIN features a short series of varied links that are joined to other repeats.

ROUND CHAIN has no front or back and the rings or links lie in two or more directions.

SIMPLE CHAIN is made from same-sized single rings or links.

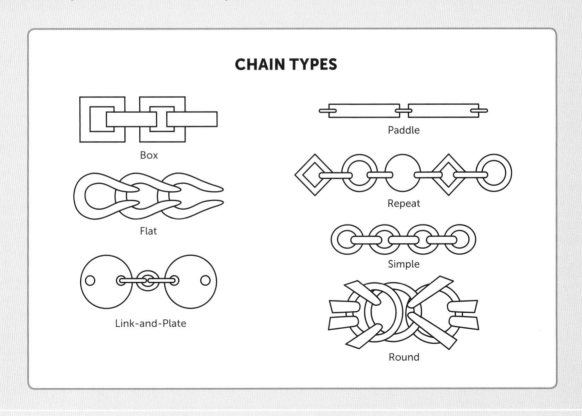

CHAIN TYPES

Box

Flat

Link-and-Plate

Paddle

Repeat

Simple

Round

APPLIED TECHNIQUE:
Make Symmetrical Fishhook Ear Wires

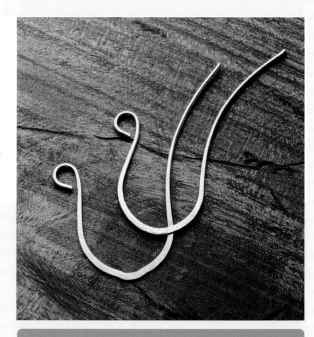

1. Cut 2 identical 3" (7.5 cm) lengths of 22-gauge sterling wire. File the cut end flush and sand the wires perfectly smooth.

2. Working with both wires at once, use small looping pliers to turn a small loop in one end of the ear wires. Keep the wires parallel as they are formed.

3. Keeping the looped wires on the pliers, finger press the center of the ear wire with your fingers around an 8 mm to 10 mm round mandrel.

4. Continue to work with the wires held parallel in the jaws of the looping pliers. Use flat-nosed pliers to create a small bend on the other end of the ear wires.

5. If desired, hammer the front segment of the ear wire flat on a steel bench block.

    Ear wire design options: Spiral ends; star ends, bent centers, squiggle wires; forged wires, paddle wires, backward wires.

Asymmetrical earring designs should be intentionally created, not an accident. The trick to earrings that match lies in shaping both wires at the same time.

BUILDING BLOCK TWELVE:
Mechanisms—Hinges, Hooks, and Other Happy Endings

TOOLS USED IN THIS SECTION:
Ring/bracelet mandrels, forming tools, rolling mill, saw frame, torch, riveting hammer, tube-cutting jig

CROSS-REFERENCES:
Filing, Abrading, and Polishing, *page 56*
Sawing and Piercing, *page 47*
Brazing and Soldering, *page 79*
Rivets, *pages 70–77*

Mechanisms and attachments make it possible for jewelry to move and to be worn on clothing or the body. These articulated elements allow jewelry items to move in one or more directions.

Mechanisms can be both functional and decorative, but it is important to create them to withstand the stress of daily wear.

Of all the fabrication processes in jewelry making, it is most important to invest the time and effort to make models and practice pieces of all types of mechanisms. After creating a practice piece, any design flaws or wearability issues can be corrected before creating the final jewelry object.

Mechanisms fall into two general categories: hinges or linkages. Hinges are one of the most beautiful and the most difficult mechanisms to fabricate in jewelry making. They are joints that move in one direction and can have a wide or narrow range of motion. Linkages are joints that can move in two or more directions and typically have a wide range of motion.

HINGES are two-sectioned mechanisms joined by a pin or rod. Interlocking sections of tubing are joined to each of the two parts and the pin is inserted into the tubing. The pin allows the hinge parts to rotate toward and away from each other. The sections of hinge tubing are called knuckles and typically, three or another odd number are required to allow a hinge to work properly. Knuckles are soldered onto the piece so the larger number is on the heavier part.

BALL-AND-SOCKET LINKAGES allow sections to move with the greatest range of motion. They can be hot- or cold-connected, but the size of the ball or other terminating feature relative to the socket is what determines the movement of the joint.

SLOT-AND-TAB LINKAGES allow movement in one or two directions. Tabs can be permanently attached or inserted into shaped slots that allow the jewelry object to be opened and closed by twisting or turning it at the linkage. Gravity secures the closure of the linkage in this style of mechanism.

HOOK-AND-LOOP LINKAGES are the main connection style for necklaces and chain. Toggles, keyhole catches, and fishhook catches fall into this category; again, gravity keeps them closed.

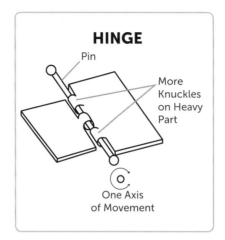

HINGE

Pin

More Knuckles on Heavy Part

One Axis of Movement

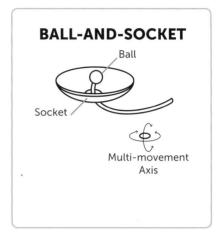

BALL-AND-SOCKET

Ball

Socket

Multi-movement Axis

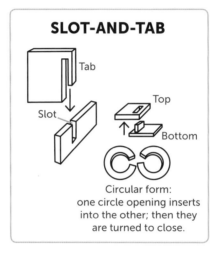

SLOT-AND-TAB

Tab

Slot

Top

Bottom

Circular form: one circle opening inserts into the other; then they are turned to close.

HOOK-AND-LOOP

Hook

Loop

APPLIED TECHNIQUE:
Sister Hook Closure

The sister hook is one of the most secure clasp designs and works well for heavy necklaces or bracelets. An added bonus is that it can usually be opened and closed without a helper.

1. Transfer the pattern to 18-gauge sterling silver sheet. Carefully saw-pierce the hook parts so they are identical.

2. Use a center punch to create a divot, then drill holes where indicated. Insert the saw blade into the drilled opening and saw-pierce the inner circle of the loop and the holes for inserting the jump rings into the closure.

3. Clean-finish all parts, sanding everything to a 600-grit finish. Polish the closure and loop.

4. Join the two halves of the hook with a running-fit rivet created from 1.63 mm OD silver tubing. Ensure the mobility of the hooks is preserved. Carefully polish the rivet.

5. Insert a 20-gauge 6mm jump ring into the drilled holes as shown; solder the ring closed with hard silver solder.

6. Attach the closure to a chain with an unsoldered jump ring.

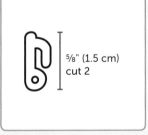

⅝" (1.5 cm)
cut 2

Actual size.

APPLIED TECHNIQUE:
Linked Bracelet with Cold-Rolled Hinges

1. Transfer the pattern to any combination of textured or untextured brass, copper, nickel, or sterling silver 20-gauge sheet. Make 6 units for an 8" (20.5 cm) bracelet. Carefully file and sand the edges of all parts, ensuring the edges of the hinge tabs are parallel and all of them are the same width so that when they are cold-rolled and left unsoldered, they fit together neatly into functioning hinge knuckles. Anneal all of the units. Quench, pickle, rinse, and dry them well: then lay them in a row the order you plan to assemble them. Note that every other link is rotated 180° to interlock at the hinge knuckles, so take the time to determine which direction is up and at the top for each link in the line. Also ensure that the tabs will slide into the adjacent link where they need to by filing them carefully until they do.

2. There are 3 design options to plan for. The inner circles of the links can be used in any combination of these options: (a) cut them out to create openings, (b) solder on discs or rings of the same diameter for overlays, or (c) fabricate bezels for 12mm round stones and solder them into position.

3. Fabricate the units with cut openings first: texture surfaces as desired, mark the openings where indicated, center-punch, and drill a pilot hole to insert the saw blade and pierce them out. Clean-finish all edges and sand every unit to a 600-grit finish. With a rawhide mallet, gently dome the link body—but not the hinge tabs. Set the textured and domed links aside, preserving their order and position in the bracelet.

There are unlimited design possibilities for creating the unit links in this bracelet. Experiment with texture, metal, adding a stone, piercing the links, or adding overlays. Tube rivets connect the links, which may be left unsoldered if desired.

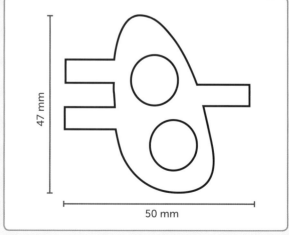

47 mm

50 mm

Actual size.

4. Fabricate the units with the sweat-soldered discs next. Plan where you will use texture, either on the overlay or the body of the link, then cut out the discs. Clean-finish the backs and edges of the discs, flux them well, and carefully sweat easy solder on the backs. Then, solder them into position on the links. Quench, pickle, and rinse well. Dry the links and, with a rawhide mallet, gently dome the link body—but not the hinge tabs, taking care to evenly dome where the soldered discs are positioned. This will also work-harden the link after soldering. Set the overlay links aside, preserving their order and position in the bracelet.

5. Fabricate the bezel units next and scribe the bezel locations on the link body. Fabricate the bezels, measuring the bezel wire for the round stones. Solder them closed with hard solder. Solder the bezels where indicated on the links with easy solder. Quench, pickle, and rinse well. Dry the links and with a rawhide mallet, gently dome the link body around the soldered bezels—but not the hinge tabs, and especially not near the bezels so as not to deform the stone settings. This will work-harden the link. Do not set the stones until the entire bracelet has been fabricated. Set the bezel links aside, preserving their order and position in the bracelet.

6. Use looping pliers to cold-roll the hinge tabs of each unit as shown to create tubing for the hinge knuckles. Test the fit of all the hinges, filing the edges of the tubing as needed to allow the links to move freely. Insert short sections of ⅛" (3 mm) brass tubing or 8-gauge brass wire to dry-fit the hinges, but do not rivet the hinge pin ends.

7. Once the entire bracelet dry-fits and the hinges move freely, remove the bezel units and set the stones. Polish and patinate the units as desired and set them aside. One by one, fit the hinge pins into the links in order. Rivet the pins into position by either flaring the edges of the brass tubing or upsetting the ends of the wire and sanding them smooth.

8. Fabricate the closure pin from 8-gauge brass wire; it should fit very tightly. Insert it into the knuckles of the last and first links to close the bracelet.

NOTE: *It is a good practice to solder the knuckles of the first and last links at the closure pin for strength and durability. At the same time, a safety chain can be soldered on or cold-connected to the last link and the end of the hinge pin to prevent loss.*

PROJECTS

These four projects will give you a chance to practice the skills you have mastered by following the applied technique exercises throughout the book.

You have the option of waiting to tackle them until after you have completed every applied technique exercise, or you may make these jewelry objects in order as you proceed through the twelve essential building blocks—as a way of reviewing what you have learned. Think of them as fabrication exams, and there is no law against do-overs!

Each of these projects focuses on an ever-increasing skillset; creating them will challenge you, but you will learn the fundamentals of jewelry fabrication if you persevere. Ultimately, you be rewarded for your patience and hard work. The joy of metalworking will be yours to enjoy for many years.

PROJECT ONE
Leaf Brooch with Saw-Pierced Fretwork
Skills: Precise sawing, pattern transfer and measuring, positioning drilled holes, rivets.

PROJECT TWO
Multilayered Riveted Pendant with Micro-Hardware
Skills: Riveting; precise sawing; filing, abrading, and polishing.

PROJECT THREE
Suite of Soldered Stack Rings from Milled Silver Stock
Skills: Material prep, measuring, sawing, filing and abrading, intermediate fabrication, forming, surface texturing, soldering, finishing and polishing.

PROJECT FOUR
Soldered Bead Collection on Fabricated Paddle Chain
Skills: Material prep, measuring, sawing, filing and abrading, advanced fabrication, forming, surface texturing, cold-connecting, soldering, patination, finishing and polishing.

Project One: *COMBINE BUILDING BLOCKS ONE, TWO, THREE, AND FIVE*

leaf brooch
with Saw-Pierced Fretwork

Skills built upon with this project:
- Precise Sawing, *pages 50–54*
- Pattern Transfer, *page 52*
- Measuring, *pages 12; 16; 32*
- Positioning Drilled Holes, *page 55*
- Rivets, *pages 70–77*

Give your jeweler's saw a workout with this project. You will learn to use a pattern, and how to cut and finish both straight and curved lines, inside openings and complex outside contours. Once you create a brooch in inexpensive brass, progress to a heavier sterling silver version for a very pretty coat pin with a high polish.

Materials
- 22-gauge brass sheet; 3" × 2" (7.5 × 5 cm)
- .020 music wire; approximately 4" (10 cm)
- Manufactured large-head rivet; 16-gauge
- Fine-tipped permanent marker
- Rubber cement
- Tripoli and rouge polishing compounds
- Saw-blade lubricant
- Liquid dish detergent

Tools
- Jeweler's saw frame
- 3/0 blades
- Scribe
- Straight edge or ruler
- Flex shaft
- Drill bits #54 and #68
- Needle files, cut 2
- Chain-, round-, and flat-nose pliers
- Riveting hammer
- Steel bench block
- Brass brush; old toothbrush
- Sanding sticks; 320-, 400-grit
- Abrasive sanding discs for flex shaft; 400 medium and 600 fine
- Hard felt polishing tips for flex shaft; 2 (1 for Tripoli, 1 for rouge)

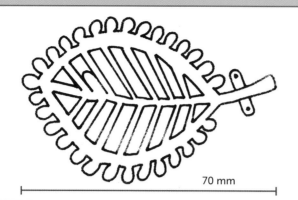

Actual size.

70 mm

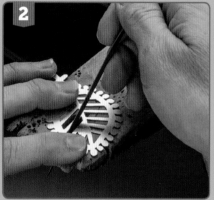

1. Clean and sand away any deep nicks or scratches from the brass sheet. Transfer the pattern to tracing paper or photocopy it. Use rubber cement to adhere the pattern firmly to the clean, dry brass sheet.

2. Using a 3/0 blade in the saw frame, trim away the perimeter, following the outer line of the pattern. It is helpful to choose either the outside or inside edge of the pattern line and saw consistently along whichever edge you choose. *(Fig. 1)*

3. Center-punch divots into all of the inner openings where indicated by red dots. Do not punch the pin catch tab or pin stem tabs at this time. Use a #54 drill bit to drill the punched divots. Carefully

insert the blade into the drilled openings and saw away the inner openings, starting in the middle and working away from the center of the brooch. After all of the openings have been sawn and the perimeter is completely sawn, remove the pattern from the sheet and scrub the metal with hot soapy water and a brass brush.

4. Refine the sawn openings with needle files, taking care not to remove too much metal. Strive for visually smooth transitions from opening to opening and uniformity in the rounded shapes along the edge of the brooch. *(Fig. 2)*

5. Once all of the sawn edges have been refined, sand the entire

brooch, the back, and all of the edges to 600-grit.

6. Center-punch the dots at the base of the pin catch section and drill them with the #68 drill bit. Use a scribe and straight edge to scribe a line on the bottom of the piece at the base of the pin stem tabs to indicate the fold line. Center-punch, but do not drill the dot on the pin stem tab. *(Fig. 3)*

7. Use wide-jaw flat-nose pliers to bend back the two tabs carefully for the pin catch. Take care not to twist the metal of the leaf stem as the tabs are formed. The tabs must be parallel to each other and perpendicular to the brooch. *(Fig. 4)*

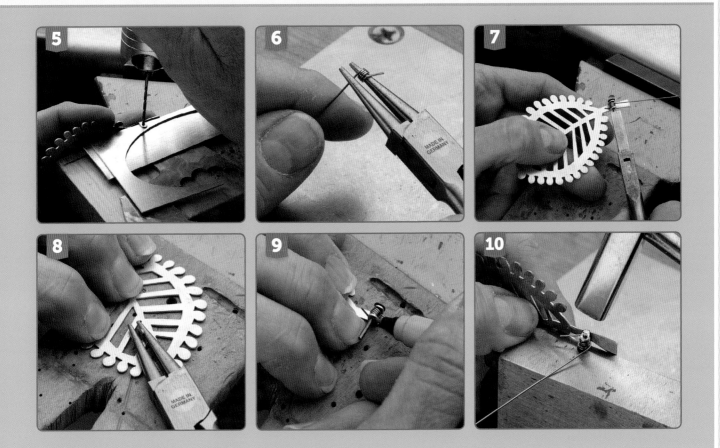

8. Use the #54 drill bit to drill the rivet hole in the pin stem tabs. Start at the center-punched divot and slowly drill through both tabs. It is helpful to support the upper tab by inserting several waste sheets of metal into the gap between the tabs as you drill. Once the top hole is drilled, remove the waste metal and use the drilled hole to guide the drilling for the other tab. *(Fig. 5)*

9. Create the spring for the pin stem by coiling the music wire around one jaw of the round-nose pliers. Leave a tail as shown to cause the spring to maintain tension against the catch as the brooch is worn. *(Fig. 6)*

10. Test-fit the rivet and the pin stem in the drilled tabs. The pin stem tail should rest flat against the back of the brooch and the stem should point straight into the air. Do not trim the pin stem wire yet. Mark the rivet wire for trimming, and remove the rivet and pin stem and set aside. *(Fig. 7)*

11. Use the center punch to push the catch gently toward the back of the brooch. Switch to round-nose pliers and create a soft loop in the catch as shown. Bring the entire brooch, both front and back, to a high polish by first polishing the entire piece with Tripoli compound. Scrub the brooch in hot soapy water with a toothbrush, dry it completely, and then polish it with rouge compound. Scrub again with hot soapy water, taking care to remove all traces of compound. Dry it completely. *(Fig. 8)*

12. Test-fit the brooch, pin stem, and catch several times, adjusting for fit and function. The pin stem should arc into the catch and not rock excessively on the rivet wire. Once everything fits well, mark the pin stem where the wire intersects the edge of the brooch. Trim it with sturdy wire cutters and sand the cut end smooth with the abrasive discs. *(Fig. 9)*

13. Trim the rivet to the indicated line and reassemble the brooch. Gently set the rivet and test the fit again. Once it is certain the rivet is positioned correctly, set the rivet carefully and planish the hammered rivet head with the large peen of the rivet hammer. Polish the entire brooch, taking care not to bend the pin stem during polishing. *(Fig. 10)*

Project Two: *COMBINE BUILDING BLOCKS THREE, FOUR, AND FIVE*

multilayered riveted pendant
with Micro-Hardware

Skills built upon with this project:

- Rivets, *pages 70–77*
- Precise Sawing, *pages 50–54*
- Filing, Abrading, and Polishing, *page 56*

Precise layout, clean saw-piercing, and good riveting techniques are essential in this project. You will cut identical shapes with varied inside openings and carefully assemble the layers to allow the play of light through the windows in the metal.

Materials

- 20-gauge aluminum sheet, 2½" × 3½" (6.5 × 9 cm)
- 26-gauge copper sheet, 2½" × 3½" (6.5 × 9 cm)
- 24-gauge brass sheet, 2½" × 3½" (6.5 × 9 cm)
- 20-gauge patterned brass sheet, 1" × 1" (2.5 × 2.5 cm)
- $3/32$" anodized-aluminum tubing, any color
- $1/16$" brass rod or 14-gauge copper wire
- Steel necklace cable with magnetic clasp
- One flat-backed drilled floral stone carving
- 2 sets 0-80 thread micro-hardware: brass or stainless-steel ½" (1.3 cm) screws and hex nuts
- Patina solution for copper
- Wax or acrylic sealer (optional)
- Rubber cement
- Superglue
- Black fine-tip permanent marker

Tools

- Jeweler's saw frame and 3/0 blades
- Disc cutter with ½" (1.3 cm) die
- Center punch
- Scribe
- Chasing or ball-peen hammer
- Riveting hammer
- Needle files, 2 and 4 cut
- Triangle needle file
- Abrasive papers, 320-, 400-, and 600-grit
- Half-round 2-cut file
- Steel bench block
- Tube-cutting jig
- Circle template or compass with scribe
- Flex shaft and abrasive discs
- Steel bristle brush for flex shaft
- #52 and #64 drill bits
- Patina brush and tray or dish
- Brass brush and liquid soap
- Millimeter gauge or ruler
- Dividers

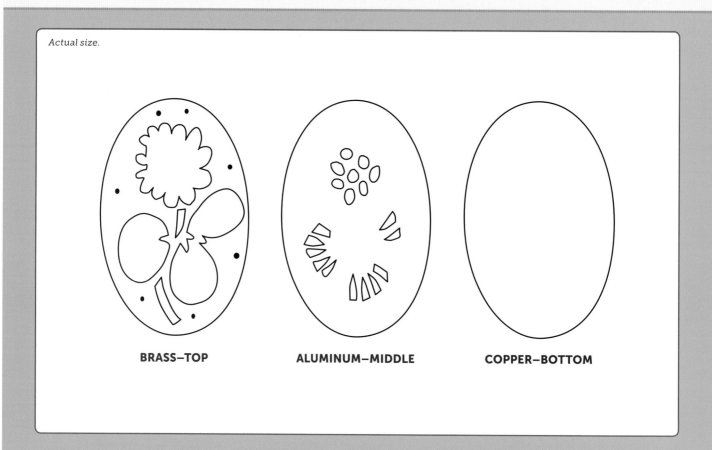

Actual size.

BRASS—TOP   **ALUMINUM—MIDDLE**   **COPPER—BOTTOM**

1. Referring to the patterns, cut 3 ovals; one each of copper, aluminum, and brass sheet. Use the half-round file and abrasive papers to clean-finish the sawn edges and smooth all surfaces of the 3 cut ovals to an uninterrupted satin finish. *(Fig. 1)* [A clean finish means filed to the sawn pattern lines and sanded; burr-free. A satin finish refers to the finish of the metal: it has to be clean, scratch-free, and sanded to an almost polish (about 600 grit).] Take care to remove all scratches and saw marks. Scrub the ovals with warm soapy water and a brass brush and set aside to dry.

   Mark 3 crosshairs on the back of the patterned brass with the fine-tip marker to indicate the center for cutting a disc and for the rivet hole. Use the marked lines for reference and cut one ½" (1.3 cm) diameter disc from the patterned brass using the disc cutter. Sand and refine all edges to remove the burr created by the cutting die, and remark the crosshair lines if needed, for positioning when filing the petals.

   Adhere the sawing patterns to the ovals with rubber cement: brass for the top layer and aluminum for the middle layer. Ensure the rubber cement is completely dry before sawing. Set the copper oval aside.

2. Use a chasing hammer and center-punch to create a divot into each area of the pattern that will be removed by saw-piercing on the top brass layer. Do not punch the rivet holes yet.

   TIP: Punch with a bench block behind the metal sheet to prevent it from deforming or denting as you strike the punch with the hammer. (Fig. 2)

3. Drill the holes for inserting the saw blade at each divot with the #52 drill bit. *(Fig. 3)*

4. Insert the blade into the drilled holes and saw out the openings of the brass layer. Work carefully in the corners and tight spots, remembering to pivot the metal carefully as the direction of sawing changes. Do not remove the pattern yet. Verify the positioning of the top brass layer over the pattern of the middle aluminum layer to ensure the pierced openings are correctly placed according to the pattern. Minor adjustments can be made if needed to the pattern position

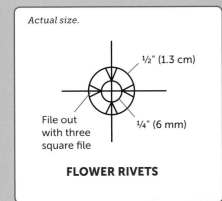

Actual size.

½" (1.3 cm)

File out with three square file

¼" (6 mm)

FLOWER RIVETS

or sawn openings of the middle layer at this time. Once the positioning is acceptable, center-punch divots into the aluminum middle-layer sawn openings as for the brass layer.

5. Gently center-punch the divots for the rivet holes in the top brass layer. Remove the pattern and sand and polish the brass to a Tripoli finish (i.e., not rouge-finished, but almost). Set aside.

   Drill the saw-blade holes into the openings of the aluminum layer with the #52 drill bit. Carefully saw away the openings, paying special attention to the direction changes in the sharp points and corners. Do not remove the pattern from the middle layer until all of the openings are sawn

and the top and middle layer positioning is checked again. Once positioning is verified, remove the pattern from the middle aluminum layer and sand the metal to a satin finish using 320-, then 400-grit abrasive paper. Refer to the pattern for the upper brass layer to position the drilled holes around the sawn openings and indicate the positions as desired with a marker dot. Gently center-punch and then drill the dots with the #64 drill bit. Sand away any burrs from the drilled holes. Set aside. *(Fig. 4)*

6. Set the tube-cutting jig to 2 mm. Cut six 2 mm sections of tubing, sanding both sawn edges of each section as they are cut. Do not sand the sides of the tubing

to avoid removing the very thin layer of color from the anodized aluminum. Set the tubing sections aside. *(Fig. 5)*

7. Gently abrade the entire surface of the copper oval with 320-grit abrasive paper. Once the copper oval is sanded, scrub it with warm soapy water and a brass brush to remove every trace of grit, oils from the skin, and tool grease. Do not touch it again with your fingers after you set it aside to dry.

   Patinate the copper to a chocolate brown or jet black, using a warm patina solution of your choice. Once the color has reached the desired level, rinse the piece well and set it aside to dry. Seal the patina with wax or acrylic sealer if desired.

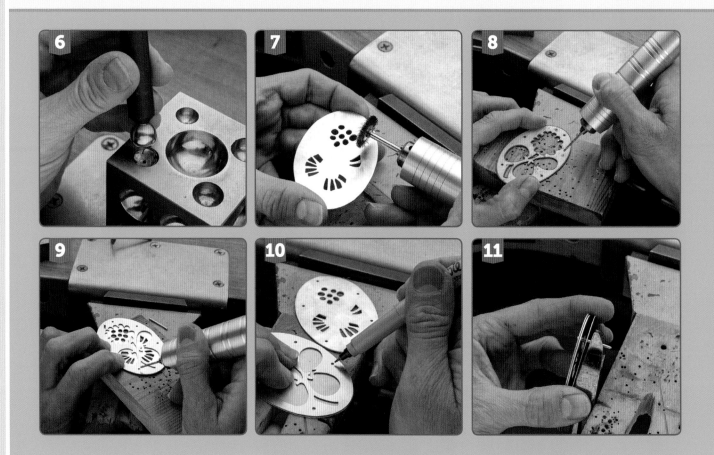

Apply several thin layers of patina and gradually build the color to the desired level, rather than try to apply a "thick" layer of color in one session. Cool the metal in an ice water "stop bath" and return it to the warm patina solution several times to build the color gradually.

8. On the back of the floral patterned disc, center and mark a ¼" (6 mm) inner circle with the fine-tip marker or a compass with a scribe tip. Nick the edge of the disc with the saw blade at each quadrant where the crosshair touches the edge. Use a triangle needle file to gently expand the sawn nick, then file 4 Vs into the disc to create petals. Do not file beyond the ¼" (6 mm) drawn line. Take care to file evenly and to create symmetrical petals. Round off any sharp corners and center-punch the intersection of the drawn lines once the filing has been completed. Sand the back of the disc smooth, then pre-polish to a Tripoli finish. Dap the disc, floral-side up, into a hemisphere. Drill the punched center with the #52 drill bit. *(Fig. 6)*

While running the power, use the steel bristle brush in the flex shaft to tap the surface of the middle aluminum layer gently to create a pebbled surface. *(Fig. 7)*

9. Drill the rivet holes with a #52 drill bit in the top brass layer: sand them smooth and remove any burrs. Bring the top layer to a high polish using jeweler's rouge on a felt wheel. Transfer the positions of the rivet holes to the middle aluminum layer with a marker. Set both layers aside. *(Fig. 8)*

10. Create 5 rivets from the ¹⁄₁₆" (2 mm) brass rod, taking care to create round, smooth, and well-shaped rivet heads. Drill one rivet hole in the middle aluminum layer and insert the first rivet into position through both layers, but do not attach it. Verify the positions of each rivet hole as they are made, drilling one at a time in the middle aluminum layer, inserting the rivet through both layers, and then moving across the piece to the opposite side to drill the next rivet hole, until all holes are drilled and the rivets or screws are positioned correctly. *(Fig. 9)*

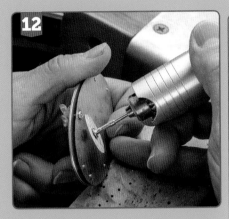

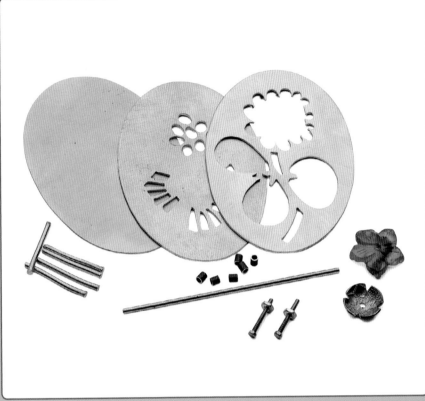

11. Once the fit of the rivet holes and relative hardware have been verified, transfer the hole positions to the bottom copper layer with a marker. As for the middle layer, center-punch and drill one hole at a time in the bottom copper layer, then position the rivets or screws accordingly through all three layers. Check and recheck the fit.

Disassemble the piece, making careful note of where each rivet goes. Polish every part carefully and check the evenness of the patina and textured surfaces prior to final assembly. *(Fig. 10)*

12. To assemble the piece, place the top layer and middle layer together. Insert the first rivet and the rivet directly opposite it through both layers. Lay the piece facedown on a steel block. Thread the tubing sections onto the rivets, then position the bottom copper layer for riveting. Trim the rivets to size with the saw, or snip them with flush cutters, taking care not to remove too much rod. File the rod, then upset the rivet head just enough to hold the layers together. ("Upset" is the term used for creating a mushroom head on a rivet or widening the edge of a metal sheet.) Do not secure the rivets until all five have been installed into the piece. *(Fig. 11)*

13. Once the rivets have been secured and the positioning is correct, set them and planish their heads with the flat face of the riveting hammer. Gently sand and polish the rivet heads on both sides of the piece. *(Fig. 12)*

14. Insert the micro-hardware through the dapped floral disc and install it through the layers in the same way as the rivets: top and middle layers, tubing, and then the bottom layer. Install the hex nut on the back, saw off the excess bolt, and tap the stub of the bolt with the riveting hammer to upset the metal and to prevent the screw from being removed. Sand the nut and bolt smooth. Repeat for the stone carving, taking care not to overtighten the screw threads or crack the stone. Add one drop of superglue to the back of each hex nut at the screw threads to prevent the nuts from being removed.

Project Three: *COMBINE BUILDING BLOCKS FOUR, SIX, SEVEN, EIGHT, AND TEN*

suite of soldered stack rings

from Milled Silver Stock

Skills built upon with this project:

- Brazing and Soldering, *page 79*
- How to Use a Bracelet or Ring Mandrel, *page 114*
- Surface Texture on Flat Sheet, *page 93*
- How to Dap a Hemisphere, *page 114*

Making a series of stackable ring bands is a fun way to stretch your measuring, fabrication, and soldering skills. Once you become familiar with the process of ring-band making, it is easy to build on those skills and begin to add gemstones to your designs.

Materials

RING A
- 10-gauge sterling silver square wire, about 2.5" (6.5 cm)
- Hard silver solder

RING B
- 16-gauge sterling silver sheet; about 2.5" (6.5 cm) × 10 mm
- One 24-gauge copper hemisphere
- Hard and medium silver solder

RING C
- 10-gauge sterling silver round wire, about 3" (7.5 cm)
- 1 small scrap of sterling silver to form granule; reserve cut end of band for this
- One 9–12 mm patterned 24-gauge sterling silver disc (left over from Applied Technique: Wire inlay between roll-patterned metal sheet, page 102)
- Hard and medium silver solder

RING D
- 6-gauge sterling silver square wire, about 80 mm
- Hard silver solder

Tools
- Millimeter gauge
- Dividers
- Steel ring mandrel
- Round wood dowel or wood mandrel
- Nylon mallet
- Torch setup: torch, flux, sharp tweezers, striker, quench, pickle pot and solution, tongs, fireproof soldering surface, soldering block, third hand or ring-soldering tripod
- Jeweler's saw frame and 2/0 blades
- Circle or disc cutter and dies
- Ring clamp
- Dapping block and punches
- Rolling mill
- Center punch
- Scribe
- Needle files, 2 and 4 cut
- Triangle needle file
- Abrasive papers: 320-, 400-, and 600-grit
- Half-round 2-cut file
- #54 drill bit
- Ball bur
- Flex shaft and abrasive discs
- Hard felt polishing tips for Tripoli and rouge polishing compounds
- Brass brush and liquid soap
- Fine-tip black permanent marker

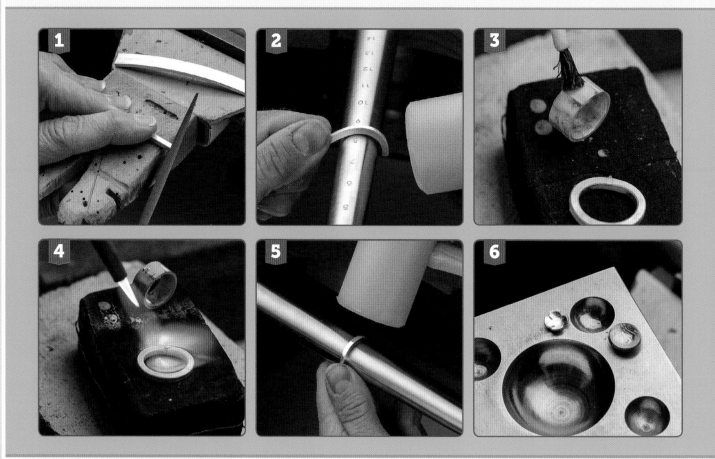

1. For each ring, determine the final ring size. Refer to the ring size chart on page 153 and prepare the metal stock for forming Rings A and B by sawing the edges clean and filing and sanding the cut edges square. Do not cut the metal stock to final size for Ring C or Ring D. *(Fig. 1)*

2. **For Ring A,** anneal and position the metal stock on the ring mandrel and hammer down the ends first using a rawhide or nylon mallet. Using the hammer, form a C-shape in the stock and gradually bring the ends together for the solder join. Do not try to create a round ring; instead, work for a perfect connection of the metal ends at the solder join. All four sides of the square stock

must match up, and the sawn edges must also line up to form as tight a fit as is possible. After soldering, the ring can be made round. Flux the band, paying particular attention to the join, and set on the soldering block. *(Fig. 2)*

3. **For Ring B,** anneal and prepare the ring band for soldering as for Ring A, again making a special effort to create a good solder join at the edges. Inspect the join very carefully and hold it up to the light to ensure there are no gaps, that the surfaces are matched, and that the cut edges of the join meet perfectly. Flux the band, paying particular attention to the join, and set on the soldering block. *(Fig. 3)*

4. In the same soldering operation, solder the join of Ring A and then Ring B. Quench in clean, clear, room-temperature water, pickle, and rinse well. Brass brush both bands to remove surface oxides, flux, and dirt. Dry both bands completely. *(Fig. 4)*

5. Form Ring A on the ring mandrel into a perfect circle by tapping it gently with the nylon mallet. Work from side to side, turning the band on the mandrel often to prevent a taper from forming. When the ring is round, has a round opening, and is the proper size, remove it from the mandrel and carefully inspect the solder join. Repair any cracks, breaks, gaps, or dips in the join by either sawing out the old solder and soldering

Ring Blanks Size Chart

Ring Sizes		B & S Sheet Metal Gauge (mm in parentheses)					
U.S.	Metric	10 (2.6)	12 (2.1)	14 (1.6)	16 (1.3)	18 (1.0)	20 (0.8)
1	39.0	47.2	45.6	44.0	43.1	42.1	41.5
2	41.5	49.7	48.1	46.5	45.6	44.6	44.0
3	44.0	52.2	50.6	49.0	48.1	47.1	46.5
4	46.5	54.7	53.1	51.5	50.6	49.6	49.0
5	49.0	57.2	55.6	54.0	53.1	52.1	51.5
6	51.5	59.7	58.1	56.5	55.6	54.6	54.0
6.5	52.8	61.0	59.4	57.8	56.9	55.9	55.3
7	54.0	62.2	60.6	59.0	58.1	57.1	56.5
7.5	55.3	63.5	61.9	60.3	59.4	58.4	57.8
8	56.6	64.8	63.2	61.6	60.7	59.7	59.1
8.5	57.8	66.0	64.4	62.8	61.9	60.9	60.3
9	59.1	67.3	65.7	64.1	63.2	62.2	61.6
9.5	60.3	68.5	66.9	65.3	64.4	63.4	62.8
10	61.6	69.8	68.2	66.6	65.7	64.7	64.1
10.5	62.8	71.0	69.4	67.8	66.9	65.9	65.3
11	64.1	72.3	70.7	69.1	68.2	67.2	66.6
11.5	65.3	73.5	71.9	70.3	69.4	68.4	67.8
12	66.6	74.8	73.2	71.6	70.7	69.7	69.1
12.5	67.9	76.1	74.5	72.9	72.0	71.0	70.4
13	69.1	77.3	75.7	74.1	73.2	72.2	71.6
13.5	71.3	79.5	77.9	76.3	75.4	74.4	73.8
14	72.6	80.8	79.2	77.6	76.7	75.7	75.1

Use this chart to calculate the sheet metal length needed for the metal gauge and finished ring size. First, find the ring size in either of the first two columns at left. Follow that row to the gauge column. Cut the metal ring blank to the millimeter length indicated.

it closed again, or pickling the ring, cleaning it well, and adding another chip of solder to the join and soldering it again. It is important to have a completely filled solder join for both durability and for appearance. Once the ring is satisfactory, gently file, sand, and pre-polish the band on the inside and outside and on all edges to a Tripoli finish. Set Ring A aside. *(Fig. 5)*

6. With the dapping block and punches, form the textured copper disc into a hemisphere roughly 9 mm wide. Form the silver disc into a hemisphere roughly 6 mm wide. Use a triangle needle file to create 4 evenly spaced indents around the perimeter of the silver disc. Clean-finish both hemispheres, sanding them to a 600-grit surface. Set aside. *(Fig. 6)*

7. Form and pre-polish Ring B as for Ring A. Make a mark at the solder join with a black marker to indicate the bottom of the ring band. With dividers, locate the center of the top of the band, and scribe crosshairs for drilling a hole in the band at the top center position. With the ring on a steel ring mandrel, use a center punch to form a small divot at the crosshairs. Move the ring band to a wood dowel or wood mandrel and drill the divot with a #54 drill bit. Use an 8 mm ball bur to carve a cup-shaped depression in the band for the copper hemisphere. Check the fit of the copper hemisphere in the cup making sure there is good contact all around and making adjustments with the ball bur for a good fit.

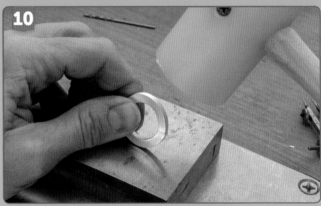

8. Position Ring B on the soldering block with the cup depression up and flux the ring well. Position the copper disc on the soldering block near the ring band and flux all surfaces well. Sweat-solder two small chips of medium solder in the cup. While the ring is still warm, position the copper cup in the depression, making sure it is level and centered. Reheat the ring until the solder flows again and joins the cup to the ring band. Quench, rinse, and pickle the ring. Inspect the solder join and once the ring is satisfactory, gently file, sand, and pre-polish the band on the inside and outside and on all edges to a Tripoli finish. Set Ring B aside. *(Fig. 7)*

9. Anneal the round wire for **Ring C** and then form it around the steel ring mandrel so the ends pass each other: the solder join will be sawn after the ring shank is perfectly round; essentially Ring C is a large jump ring. Once the proper size has been formed, draw a perpendicular line across both coils of the wire and saw out through both wires at the overlap forming a perfect, giant jump ring. Reserve the cutoffs to form the granule and stem.

10. Using two pairs of chain-nose pliers, gently bring the wire ends together so they meet in a tight join for soldering, taking care not to mar the wire with the pliers. Solder the band closed as for Ring A and clean-finish it to a 600-grit finish. Indicate the solder join with the marker for the bottom of the band as for Ring B.

11. Using the reserved cutoffs, cut one 5 mm section for the stem, file the ends square, and carve a depression in the end of the wire with the 8 mm ball bur for the silver hemisphere. In the other end of the wire, file a gentle curve for the solder join. It is essential to match the curve of the ring band for a sound join. *(Fig. 8)*

12. Flux the other cutoff completely, position it on the soldering block, and heat it until the metal reaches liquidus and pulls together into a flat-bottomed sphere. Allow the granule to cool completely, then pickle it well, rinse, and return it to the solder block. Sweat-solder a small chip of medium solder in the base of the silver hemisphere. While the metal is still hot, use sharp tweezers to position the granule in the hemisphere and

heat until the solder reflows to join the granule to the hemisphere. Quench, then pickle, rinse, and dry. Clean-finish the flower assembly to a 600-grit finish.

13. Solder the stem to the ring band with medium solder. Quench, pickle, rinse, and dry. Bring the soldered ring to a Tripoli pre-polish and wash the ring in hot soapy water. Position the ring with the stem up on the solder block. Position the flower assembly on the block and flux the bottom well. Flux the entire ring and place a chip of medium solder in the burred depression in the top of the stem. Heat the ring until the solder flows. While still hot, use sharp tweezers to position the flower assembly in the depression,

taking care to ensure it is centered and level. Heat the ring until the solder reflows, joining the flower to the stem. Quench, pickle, rinse, and dry. Bring Ring C to a Tripoli finish and set aside. *(Fig. 9)*

14. For **Ring D,** anneal the 6 mm square metal stock and roll it in the flat side of the rolling mill so it measures 4.5 mm x about 3.9 mm. Form the ring around the mandrel with a nylon mallet, making a special effort to get a narrow and clean soldering join. It is critical to have a strong, well-soldered, and completely full-solder fillet, so take the time and anneal as often as needed to get a good join. Try not to mar the metal to save finishing work later in the process. Saw the kerf

for the join cleanly from the inner opening of the ring outward with a 2/0 blade. Then tap the ring ends together with a nylon mallet. Solder the ring with plenty of hard solder and inspect the join for completeness. *(Fig. 10)*

15. Reshape Ring D on the mandrel and take the time to ensure it is completely round, even, sanded smooth, and polished to a Tripoli finish. Use dividers to double-check and scribe the final width of the band. Hand-file to the scribed outline so the ring is perfectly even and round. *(Fig. 11)*

16. Bring all four rings to a brilliant mirror polish using red rouge on a hard felt wheel. *(Fig. 12)*

Project Four: *COMBINE BUILDING BLOCKS SIX, SEVEN, AND EIGHT*

soldered bead collection

on Fabricated Paddle Chain

Skills built upon with this project:

- Brazing and Soldering, *page 79*
- How to Use a Bracelet or Ring Mandrel, *page 114*
- Surface Texture on Flat Sheet, *page 93*

Combine surface texturing, simple metal forming, fabrication, and soldering all in one project. This final unit project draws upon all the skills you have practiced so far.

Materials

- Copper and brass sheet 20- to 24-gauge
- .375 x .064 copper strip
- Hard and easy solder, flux
- 10-gauge copper square wire for paddle links
- 16-gauge brass wire for jump rings
- Liver of sulfur or other patina for copper and copper alloys

Tools

- Rolling mill and/or hand-texturing tools (hammers, punches, stamps)
- 1" (2.5 cm) disc cutter
- Steel ring mandrel; or round mandrel approximately ⅞" (2.2 cm) diameter
- Mandrel for jump ring, 4–4.5 mm
- Nylon mallet
- Torch and soldering setup (see Brazing, page 79 for detailed list)
- Quench and pickle pots
- Flex shaft and #52 drill bit
- Tumbler with steel shot and polishing compound or sanding and polishing tips for the flex shaft
- Sandpaper: 600-grit
- Half-round file
- Circle template
- Saw frame and 2/0 saw blade
- Round-nose pliers
- Chain-nose pliers, 2 pairs
- Solder-cutting pliers
- Flush cutters, heavy duty
- Center punch
- Fine-tip permanent marker
- Brass brush
- Dish liquid
- Baking soda
- Paper towels
- Ruler

1. Anneal the copper or brass sheet as needed, then pattern the surface of the annealed metal by either direct texturing with hand tools or by indirect transfer of the pattern using the rolling mill to emboss the metal. Do not roll the metal thinner than 26 gauge. *(Fig. 1)*

2. Use the disc cutter to cut two 1" (2.5 cm) patterned metal discs per bead. Cut one 76 to 77 mm length of the copper strip for each bead. Clean-finish all parts to remove any burr left by the disc cutter and ensure the cut ends of the copper strip are flat, clean, and perpendicular for soldering. Anneal: quench, pickle, and rinse the copper strips. Dry them completely. *(Fig. 2)*

3. On the mandrel, mallet the copper strip into a ring, paying careful attention to the join—it is critical to have a strong, even, and tight seam for the solder to flow completely and to fill the opening. The ring can be rounded after soldering, so focus attention on the seam, not the overall shape of the ring. Solder the ring closed with plenty of hard solder and inspect the fillet after soldering to ensure there are no gaps or indentations. Quench, pickle, rinse, and dry the soldered ring. Round it on the mandrel and carefully file away any errant solder that might mar the surface of the copper. *(Fig. 3)*

4. Use the circle template to indicate the stringing holes. Position the solder join at 9 or 3 o'clock and the drilling holes at 12 and 6 o'clock. Indicate the center of the width of the metal strip with a marker line to create crosshairs for drilling. Center-punch and drill the holes with the #52 drill bit. Carefully sand away any burrs created in the drilling process. The holes must be drilled before soldering the bead closed, so do not skip this step at this time. *(Fig. 4)*

5. Set a patterned disc facedown on the soldering surface and flux the back. Flux the soldered ring generously and then position the ring on the center of the disc. There should be no overlap. Cut several pallions of easy solder and position them on the inside of the bead adjacent to the base of the wall created by the soldered ring. Heat the bead until the solder flows and quench the work once the red glow has gone from the metal. Quench, pickle well, rinse, and use a brass brush lubricated with dish liquid to scrub away any surface oxides from the metal. Rinse and dry. *(Fig. 5)*

6. Set the bead on the block with the open side up and flux it well. Have the second disc fluxed and ready to lay on the bead.

Sweat-solder a few chips of easy solder on the top of the ring where it will be joined to the other disc. After the solder has flowed and while the piece is still warm, lay the other disc on the bead and heat the join until the sweated solder reflows. Once the red glow is gone from the metal, carefully quench the bead in water with the hole facing up. Repeat this process for the remaining 5 beads. *(Fig. 6)*

7. Pickle all of the beads and remove them once the black oxides have cleared the surface of the copper. With the brass brush and dish liquid, scrub them all clean. Rinse and dry. Patinate with warm liver of sulfur solution or a patina of your choice. Once the desired color has been achieved, drop the beads into a bowl of warm water mixed with baking soda to soak overnight (4 tablespoons [59.15 ml] of soda to a cup of water). This will neutralize any lingering pickle or patina that might be trapped inside the beads. Rinse and dry them well, with the holes facing down on paper towels. *(Fig. 7)*

8. Saw fourteen 1" (2.5 cm) sections of the 10-gauge square wire. Clean-finish all of the wire ends with a file and sandpaper to remove any burrs left from sawing. Anneal the wire sections, quench, and pickle them well. Scrub off the oxides with a brass brush and dish liquid. Rinse and dry them completely. *(Fig. 8)*

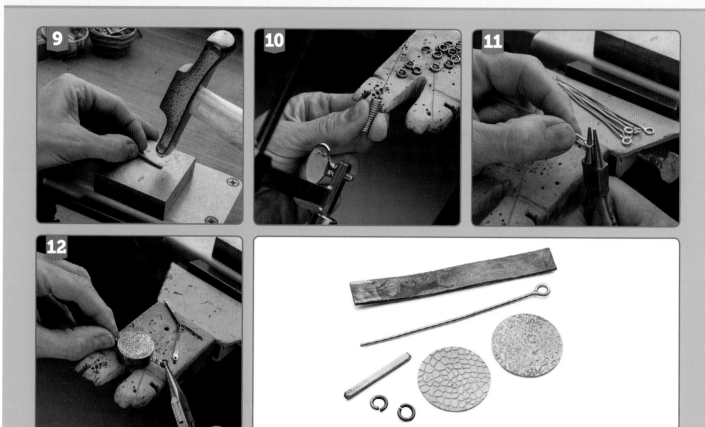

9. Hammer one end of each wire into a flat paddle about 5 mm wide. Rotate the wire 90°, then hammer a flat paddle on the other end of each wire. Use a center punch and the #52 drill bit to drill a hole in the hammered end of each paddle link. Clean up the links, remove any burrs from drilling, and sand each to a 600-grit finish. Set the finished links aside. *(Fig. 9)*

10. Create a coil of 8 mm OD jump rings from the 16-gauge brass wire. Saw them apart with a 2/0 blade and carefully sand away any remaining burrs. Using two pairs of chain-nose pliers, join the paddle chain links with the jump rings into two 7-link-long sections. You may solder the rings closed with easy solder once the chain sections have been assembled, or leave them cold connected because the brass wire will work-harden rapidly, leaving little danger of the links accidently opening. Patinate the chains with warm liver of sulfur and then tumble or hand-polish each link to remove excess patina selectively. Set the sections aside. *(Fig. 10)*

11. Cut six 3" (7.5 cm) lengths of 16-gauge brass wire. File the ends flush and form a loop in one end of each wire with round-nose pliers to create an eye pin. Flux the wires and place a chip of solder on each one at the intersection of the loop and the wire stem. Solder the joins closed one by one, quench them, and drop the wires into the pickle. *(Fig. 11)*

12. To assemble the bead links, string each bead on an eye pin. Either form a wire wrap on the unsoldered end of the wire; or use round-nose pliers to form loops identical to the other side of the bead, then solder them closed with easy solder, quench them, and drop them into the pickle.

Assemble the necklace with the remaining jump rings, joining the 6 beads together in the center of the necklace and attaching the chain sections to the first and last beads at either side. Add a commercially made clasp, or fabricate one yourself. *(Fig. 12)*

GLOSSARY

ALLOYS Metal "mixtures"; precious metal alloy formulas are regulated by law for purity control.

ANNEAL To return work-hardened metal to a malleable state.

ANODIZE To apply a colored oxide to a metal surface using electric current.

ANTICLASTIC A saddle-shaped curve.

BASE METAL Industry term for nonprecious metals used for jewelry making.

BASKET SETTING A common pronged stone setting that resembles a basket.

BI-METALS Two distinct metals or alloys that are bonded together without the use of solder.

BURNISHER A smooth steel tool used to remove imperfections from the surface of jewelry metal.

BUR; BURIN; GRAVER A motorized tip or hand-cutting tool.

BURR A ridge or curl of metal produced during sawing or drilling.

BYPASS RING A nonsoldered ring that exploits the strength of work-hardening the metal during forming. The bypass can be horizontal, vertical, or diagonal.

CABOCHON Flat-backed, domed stone.

CAMEO A carved gemstone that typically features a raised, realistic scene.

CLEAN-FINISH To create a smooth, precise, and defect-free part or component.

CULET The pointed bottom of a faceted stone.

CURVILINEAR FILE Riffler file.

CUTTING DIE A sharpened steel tool that can be used to cut regular, repeatable shapes.

DIGITAL CALIPERS battery operated measuring device.

DIVIDER Simple but useful tool that is used to set a measurement.

DIVOT A small impression typically used for centering.

END-HOOK STAKE A forming tool shaped like a hook.

ENGRAVING BALLS A sophisticated vise that relies on pegs and tension to hold work steady.

ESCAPEMENT FILE A very small, finely cut file for precise metal removal.

EUROSTYLE A ring band that features a wide-bottomed shape for comfort.

FABRICATION Construction of metal parts to create jewelry.

FERROUS AND NONFERROUS METAL Metals that contain iron or steel; metals that do not contain iron or steel.

FILLED METALS A core of one metal surrounded by a layer of another, usually precious metal.

FILLET A thin plug or seam of solder.

FINDING Attachment device used to connect a part to a part, or a jewelry object to the wearer or wearer's clothing.

FLEX SHAFT A motorized tool used with attachments that drill, cut, sand, or polish jewelry materials.

FRETWORK Open areas sawn into metal sheet.

GAUGE The standard thickness of metal sheet or wire.

GIRDLE The "waist" of a faceted gemstone.

GRAVER A very sharp hand-cutting tool.

GYPSY SETTING Old term for a flush stone setting.

INGOTS Metal bars of standard weight.

INNER DIAMETER (ID) A measurement for the inside of a circular or tubular form.

INTAGLIO A carved gemstone that features an incised scene.

JEWELER'S BRONZE A modern alloy of copper and other metals used in lieu of traditional bronze, which contains a greater amount of tin.

KERF The opening created by a saw blade or other cutting tool.

KEUM-BOO Gold bonded to fine silver.

KNUCKLES The tubular sections of a hinge.

LAPIDARY The art of cutting or carving stone.

LEMEL Filings, shavings, and dust created during metalworking.

LIQUIDUS The temperature at which solid metal changes to a liquid state; each metal differs.

MAILLE Connected rings of metal that form a fabric-like mesh.

MICRO-SPICULUM BLOCK A tiny forming block used to create tapered tubes.

MILLED STOCK Commercially created metal used as a starting point for jewelry making.

MOKUMÉ-GANE A metal created by bonding layers of different metal sheet into one billet. The technique was invented in Japan.

MONEL METAL An alloy of nickel and copper, with some iron and other trace elements.

NOBLE METAL Metals that are resistant to corrosion and oxidation in moist air.

OUTER DIAMETER (OD) The measurement of the outside of a circular tube or form.

OXIDE Rust or other visual evidence on metal of a chemical reaction caused by exposure to moist air.

PATINATION Purposeful application of oxides to metals.

PAVÉ SETTING "Paved" gemstones; a style of setting that positions multiple faceted gems very closely so they appear to cover the metal surface with stone.

PICKLING Removal of oxides from metal using acid.

PILOT HOLE A tiny diameter hole in metal used to center and guide progressively larger cutting tools.

PRECIOUS METAL; *see* noble metal.

PRONG SETTING A style of gemstone setting that features tiny clawlike sections of metal that encircle the stone.

REACTIVE METAL All metals are reactive; some like aluminum, niobium and titanium, react predictably when anodized and are loosely grouped under this industry term.

REFRACTORY METAL Refractory metals are very resistant to heat and wear .

REPOUSSÉ A technique used to decorate metal sheet by pushing it into relief with punches and hammers.

RETICULATION SILVER An 80/20 alloy of silver and copper.

RUB-OVER SETTING A bezel.

SCRIBE A very sharp marking tool.

SETTING STICKS Flat-topped tools used with wax to secure a jewelry object during stone setting.

SINUSOIDAL STAKE A snakelike metal forming tool.

SOLDER; SOLDERING Joining metal parts by melting a similar metal (solder) and introducing it into the "seam" between various parts.

SPOT PRICE The daily worldwide cost of an ounce of a particular metal.

SPRING DIVIDER; CALIPER; DIVIDER A device used to measure the distance between two opposite sides of an object.

SPUR A raised, pointed curl of metal.

STONE SEAT A cut area within a setting that allows a gemstone to be positioned for both security and beauty.

SWARF The raised curl of metal created by a graver or other cutting or scraping tool.

SYNCLASTIC A bowl-shaped curve.

TABLE The flat top of a faceted gemstone.

TENSION SETTING A prongless style of gemstone setting that relies on only the tensile strength of the metal to secure the gem.

THERMOPLASTIC Polymer that becomes pliable or moldable when heated above a specific temperature and returns to a solid state when cool.

TINNING; SWEAT SOLDERING Coating a metal part with solder prior to joining it to another part.

TRANSITIONAL METAL Any element in the d-block of the periodic table of elements.

TROY WEIGHT Unit of mass used for precious metals. There are 12 troy ounces per troy pound rather than the 16 of the common avoirdupois system. A troy ounce is 480 grains.

TUBE SETTING A style of rub-over setting or bezel that is used for round faceted stones.

RESOURCES
for Tools & Materials

Suppliers

Allcraft Jewelry Supply Co.
135 W. 29th St., Ste. 205
New York City, NY 10001

Hard-to-find imported hand tools, forming hammers, fine and base metals, and supplies.

PHONE: (800) 645-7124
or (212) 279-7077
WEB: www.allcraftusa.com
EMAIL: allcrafttools@yahoo.com
STORE PICKUP: Call (212) 279-7077
or visit 9:00 a.m. to 5:00 p.m. ET,
Monday through Friday.

Metalliferous
34 W. 46th St.
New York, NY 10036

Tools, equipment, metals, vintage component, solutions, and Thompson Enamels.

MAIL ORDER: 640 S. Fulton Ave.
Mount Vernon, NY 10550
PHONE: (212) 944-0909
or (914) 664-3300
TOLL FREE: (888) 944-0909
FAX: (914) 664-3778
WEB: store.metalliferous.com
EMAIL: info@metalliferous.com

Otto Frei
126 2nd St.
Oakland, CA 94607

Quality supplies, equipment and Platinum and 18K findings for the professional jeweler. Imported tools from Switzerland, Germany, Italy, England, Japan, and France.

PHONE: (800) 772-3456 M–F,
8:30 a.m. to 5:00 p.m. PT
FAX: (800) 900-3734 or (510) 834-6217
BUSINESS LINE: (510) 832-0355
WEB: www.ottofrei.com
EMAIL: info@ottofrei.com

Rio Grande
7500 Bluewater Rd. NW
Albuquerque, NM 87121

Comprehensive full-service supplier; 24/7 online ordering. Large inventory of tools, equipment, fine metals, gemstones and supplies.

TOLL-FREE: (800) 545-6566
TOLL-FREE FROM CANADA, PUERTO RICO AND THE U.S. VIRGIN ISLANDS: (800) 253-9738
TOLL-FREE FROM MEXICO: 95-800-253-9738
FAX: (505) 839-3016
WEB: www.riogrande.com
EMAIL: info@riogrande.com

Stuller, Inc.
302 Rue Louis XIV
Lafayette, LA 70508

Quality gemstones, fine metals and findings, quality tools. Wholesale only to qualified members of the jewelry trade. Account qualification required for pricing or ordering.

PHONE: (800) 877-7777
TOLL-FREE: (800) 444-4741
FAX: (800) 444-4741
BUSINESS OR INTERNATIONAL:
(337) 981-1655
WEB: www.stuller.com

Instructional DVDs

Metalsmith Essentials: Basic Fabrication, Helen I. Driggs (Interweave, 2011).

Metalsmith Essentials: Create Spirals, Tubes, and Other Curves for Jewelry Making, Helen I. Driggs (Interweave, 2013).

Metalsmith Essentials: Machine Finishing Jewelry, Helen I. Driggs (Interweave, 2012).

Metalsmith Essentials: Riveting and Cold Connections, Helen I. Driggs (Interweave, 2011).

Metalsmith Essentials: Textures and Patinas, Helen I. Driggs (Interweave, 2011).

INDEX

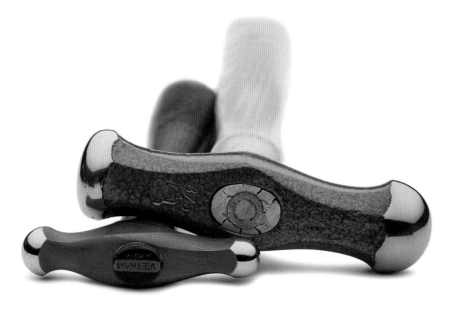

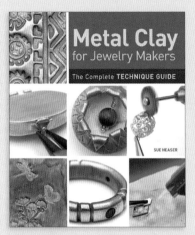